REBEL
——— AT ———
WORK

REBEL

—— AT ——

WORK

How to Innovate and Drive Results
When You Aren't the Boss

NATALIE NEELAN

DIVERSION
BOOKS

Diversion Books
A Division of Diversion Publishing Corp.
443 Park Avenue South, Suite 1004
New York, NY 10016
www.diversionbooks.com

www.natalieneelan.com

For more information, email info@diversionbooks.com

First Diversion Books edition June 2018.
Paperback ISBN: 978-1-63576-399-7
eBook ISBN: 978-1-63576-398-0

LSIDB/1804

This book is dedicated to my dysfunctional family. ;)

Contents

Preface

IN AMERICAN BUSINESS CULTURE, THE EMPHASIS PLACED BY leaders and lower-level employees about how to cooperate doesn't seem to be nearly as important as how to dominate. It's time to change that. There is nothing wrong with healthy competition. But when people are competing for themselves over the benefit of one's team, you don't have collaboration, you have dysfunction.

No one should have to endure working in a dysfunctional environment just to pay the bills. It isn't enough to survive at work, accepting that we are powerless to change the status quo. New tools and mindsets are necessary to alter the course.

I am not a culture expert. I am not a paid speaker. I am a frustrated Rebel of the status quo who has a message to share. I want you to refine the concepts I put forth in this book and then build upon them. Take what you like and throw out what you don't.

I did not write this book for money. I wrote this book for you—a hard worker who is treated like a minion in a company where self-serving behavior and wheel spinning is crushing your spirit. I wrote this for anyone who is tired of banging their heads up against the same brick wall trying to advance their careers. I wrote this because books like this don't exist, and we, the "minions," need to find a way to feel proud of our contribution to the world.

From a moral and ethical perspective, I wrote this book to encourage us to stop and reconsider the profit-at-all-cost-related decisions we make at work every day. It is one thing to create value for a customer; it is another thing to hold customers over a barrel for every penny that can be plucked from their pockets. It's one thing to employ people to work toward the goals of the company. It is another thing when those employees are treated as disposable or as cost to be cut to maximize shareholder value.

I wanted to see if I could channel the negative feelings that develop from working in dysfunctional environments into something more positive. I wanted to see if I could create solutions to accelerate the adoption of change in risk-resistant cultures. There had to be a solution for the interactions that make our souls sick.

Are you burnt out trying to do your job because of the negativity of your workplace? Do you feel held back because of people and their agendas? Are you meant to contribute to the world in a much more meaningful way?

If so, read on. You are about to permanently transform the way you look at your colleagues, your contributions, and your ability to change the world for the better.

CHAPTER 1

Do You Even Know What You Are up Against at Work?

I used to work for a fantastic company. We were encouraged to work cross-functionally. Now they call it "matrix" or "lattice" or "cross-collaboration." Back then, it was called working as a team.

Everyone was treated with respect for the value that they could deliver to the business. It had nothing to do with a title. Everyone's role contributed to the collective success of the company.

The level of trust was high throughout the organization because of the belief our leaders had in us. When an SVP introduced us to a business contact, there was a transference of trust. Confidence compounded with each new introduction and made business enjoyable.

Our leaders would allow us to solve both big and small problems. It was okay if potential solutions failed. That was the way we would learn, both about the issue and the way we were approaching our solution. We rose to the challenge and figured out a solution together. Ideas were never stifled because new ideas were the growth engine of the business.

Solving the puzzle of how to create value for our customers was the reward. Our satisfaction came from the mental challenge of cracking the code. The cooperative approach took competitiveness out of the mix. We enlisted the help of our peers and competed against the goals we set for ourselves. We were all successful because we shared a sense of purpose. We didn't need a financial incentive (although it was nice).

Tim, an associate merchant at a clothing retailer, had a similar experience. *"I have worked on great teams in the past. It reminded me of playing on great sports teams in my youth. We all trusted each other and looked out for each other. We picked each other up when we made mistakes or needed help. We all worked for the same common goal and kept it in mind at all times. We had each other's backs and always came to a stout resolution. Fighting and bickering was minimal, and there was no politicking or nonsense."*

I was happy writing about my old company. It brought back memories of fun times and some of the best leadership lessons of my life.

When you work within a company like this, count your lucky stars. You are one of the fortunate who feels supported and appreciated. In turn, you can take that positive energy to encourage others to be their best too. Great cultures do exist because of people like you. The lessons in this book will propel you and your team to even greater success.

If you don't work in a functional company like this, you will want to keep reading as well. I recognize your invisible scars from banging your head up against that corporate brick wall. We are bonded because of our common battles against the status quo.

I know a new way to survive and thrive in a dysfunctional culture that is less stressful and gets results. Follow me.

WORKPLACE STRESS HAS VERY HIGH COSTS

Today, companies are wildly profitable, but employees work harder than ever. Workplace stress is responsible for up to $190B in annual U.S. healthcare costs. Employees work with formidable bosses, stressed out coworkers, and job insecurity daily.

Would you believe that workplace depression and PTSD are actual diagnoses from work-related stress? What's worse is that workplace stressors don't necessarily have to impact an employee directly. The toll of witnessing others being bullied or watching the leaders of an organization bend the rules results in the same sick feelings amongst employees—second-hand stress.

Dysfunction also affects another critical aspect of a company— the quality of its products and services.

> *"In a 2015 study published in the Journal of Pediatrics, twenty-four teams of doctors and nurses specializing in neonatal intensive care at four hospitals in Israel participated in a simulation that involved a preterm infant (a mannequin) suffering from a medical complication. The teams were randomly assigned to receive rude treatment—an 'expert' from the U.S. made disparaging remarks, suggesting that they 'wouldn't last a week' in his department—or neutral treatment.*
>
> *'The results were scary,' says Dr. Erez. 'The teams exposed*

to rudeness gave the wrong diagnosis, didn't resuscitate or ventilate appropriately, didn't communicate well, gave the wrong medications and made other serious mistakes.'"*

We all need to feel safe and useful to our teams at work. But when members of that team put us down, or ignore us (or others), our thoughts turn from the work at hand to the actions of the person making us feel terrible. It's all we can think of. We rehash our negative experience with the offending party and project what our future interactions—with them, and with others—will look like. The negative feelings cycling inside our mind create a ripple effect with those we engage with during the course of our day. When we are on edge, our negative energy rubs off on our colleagues.

People who are on power trips, or do the least amount of work possible, impact productivity and morale. Ultimately, people end up paying to work in corporate America with their physical and mental health. The overall spending, for companies and individuals, on mental, emotional, and physical healthcare skyrockets.

THE TRUTH ABOUT CORPORATE INERTIA

Corporate inertia describes companies that have become complacent in their business methods and just cruise along.

There are two types of corporate inertia:

1. Companies with few competitors and a limited churn of customers

---

* Wallace, J. (2017, August 18). The Costs of Workplace Rudeness. Retrieved from Wall Street Journal: https://www.wsj.com/articles/the-costs-of-workplace-rudeness-1503061187

2. Companies with many competitors and a high churn of customers

Whether your corporate treadmill runs on a low setting or a high setting, the constant mile per hour pace is the inertia.

FEW COMPETITORS AND LIMITED CHURN OF CUSTOMERS

Consumers trust the big brands. Household names equal trust, which is transferred from generation to generation. When a company with few competitors and low customer turnover is entrenched in the existing way of doing business, there is no sense of "hurry up" to create new value. There is no need to rush or change anything because politics trump productivity. Busy work is the norm, and the bureaucracy sustains the mediocrity.

Kevin, a partner in a large consultancy, said, *"Complacency is rampant in corporate America. Just about anyone that has spent any amount of time 'within the walls' has seen this first hand. Overinflated, mature companies. They are breeding grounds for this type of behavior."*

Companies grew, and continue to grow, to be so big that employees play it safe. They operate under the mindset that they just need to maintain what they do every day, plus enough to earn their raise and bonus. Employees focus on incremental add-ons to meet the objectives of contributing to the growth of the department. But they're careful not to exceed those objectives, lest their goals next year require more effort to attain.

The mission for individual employees is not to screw up in these large companies. This avoidance of doing their very best translates into the entire organization striving to achieve the status quo.

MANY COMPETITORS AND A HIGH CHURN OF CUSTOMERS

When your company has many competitors, with customers who abandon ship thanks to lower prices or novelty, you simply trade accounts with those competitors.

Your team may have worked overtime to acquire a company from your competitor this year. A huge win. But you probably lost a customer to them as well. Don't worry, you can trade again next month or next year.

This is another form of corporate inertia. No matter how difficult it is to secure a customer, you end up running as hard as you can to stay in place, year over year. You lose them as fast as you sign them, working that extra 3 percent to satisfy the shareholders.

When there are losses in a highly competitive industry with a high churn of customers, the answer from leadership is, "Push the employees harder." Losses in these types of companies are typically managed month to month or by the quarter. The focus is always reactionary based on the numbers of the day.

Marc, a help desk administrator, explains, *"The workload exceeds the capacity of employees. We all sacrifice family time, our health, we are all on anti-anxiety meds, and we work weekends to meet service level agreements. Management is aware of all of this and has stated that there will be no changes."*

When company demands are extraordinary, the direction at the department level changes almost daily. These changes create uncertainty and fear. Fear of losing one's employment, or goals doubling, layer onto an already stressful day-to-day job. "Do more with less," is the company mantra. Work overtime, for free.

Mary, a claims adjuster, told me, *"Management doubled their number of staff while us underlings were told that we could have our title elevated. The elevated title means more work and more responsibility, but they will not compensate us for it because they are trying to 'do more with less.' We are gouging our customers with price increases, and our executive leaders are getting millions in bonuses. There is something seriously wrong. We don't have a real voice in stopping management from doing this stuff. It all falls on deaf ears."*

When people feel the pressure to meet goals no matter what, they cut corners and try to max out opportunities, ethical or not. The mission for individual employees is to survive today and deal with tomorrow later.

DYSFUNCTIONAL INERTIAL HYBRID

In many companies, you have both scenarios at various levels of the organization and in different departments. Perhaps there is no sense of "hurry up" on the top, and panic and chaos on the bottom. Or vice versa. Also, different departments of coworkers can demonstrate these hybrid qualities.

Nothing changes if bonuses are paid. Corporate inertia floats the boat. But don't worry. Your competition rides on the current of inertia too. It is the American corporate treadmill.

In a dysfunctional environment, you can fall into despair expecting nothing to change. Others' acceptance of this inertia intensifies how you feel. Inertia is an infection inside of a company. Once people witness inertia, it has the potential to become a chronic condition. Some seek to control it by exercising power. Some attempt to pass the buck and just avoid challenging work because they can.

Adopting "best practices" means that people don't think of new solutions for themselves. They don't have to think. Someone already did the thinking for them. We follow this derivative reasoning blindly, rising to the level of industry mediocrity.

Here is the thing that is horrible about inertia—it kills thinking. It kills organic growth. For individuals, it destroys the feeling of creating something meaningful and feeling fulfilled. Inertia ruins a person's sense of purpose.

THE BIG DELUSION

Lots of corporate leaders claim that they want to be on the "cutting edge," that they want to "disrupt." But, the corporate machine likes conformity, trade secrets, efficiency, matching results to forecasts using Six Sigma efficiencies, and "doing more with less" to improve profit margins. They want the success without the risks and work that is required to evolve.

As a result, to convince the people who hold positional power over you to do things in a new way isn't a happy experience. It is a grinding, protracted battle.

This nature of wanting conformity and needing change are two conflicting approaches that are at odds from the get-go.

THOSE WHO GET IT DONE

Who is driving the change in the great companies of the world?

Rebels. Rebels like you.

You rebel against corporate inertia. You resist against the status quo. Passionate Rebels like you who want to change things for the better are immune to the inertia contagion. You see the purpose of putting your mind to the task to find new ways to solve challenging problems. You aren't afraid to fail and learn from mistakes when seeking a better way forward. You aren't afraid to give credit to others when it is their ideas, not yours, that solve the problems. It is people like you who change the inertia.

Rebels like you don't relax with groups or communities that seek the safety of business-as-usual. You want to transform business-as-usual. You put the treadmill in motion in a functional company.

But in a dysfunctional company, your efforts are thwarted. The problem is that you are running uphill, on the treadmill, into a hurricane headwind, with a parachute of conformity trailing behind you.

CHAPTER 2

What You Should Know About Corporate Conformists

CONTRIBUTING YOUR PERSONAL BEST BRINGS YOU FULFILLMENT. That feeling is much more satisfying than any company "perk." When your work combines with the work of like-minded others, you serve the world. This picture represents a functional company.

When I address dysfunction, I'm talking about the people inside of your company who hinder your work because of their selfish motivations. Dysfunctional behavior is enacted by people who purposely dismiss your input, fail to involve you, stall on decisions, make rash decisions, or even just fail to do what they are supposed to do. Dysfunctional behaviors derail your progress at work.

Toxic behavior is more poisonous and more harmful in its

effects. Cheating, stealing, scheming, lying, and selfish decisions impact your productivity and disturb you when you see them taking place.

When these negative behaviors are exhibited by more people in your company than the positive and productive behaviors of Rebels, you have what you might think of as a dysfunctional company culture.

But it isn't the company culture in and of itself. It is the 10 percent of dysfunctional individuals who are distributed throughout the company that become the problem. You need to navigate somehow around these folks to get anything accomplished. That navigation requires driving your initiatives when it makes sense and holding your breath when it is dangerous to proceed.

When a Corporate Conformist is your boss, or bosses of departments that touch your work, you need different approaches to innovating and driving results. However, you also need the same methods for your Corporate Conformist peers or direct reports.

Advancing ideas inside of a company that is rife with dysfunction created by Corporate Conformists is like scuba diving with sharks with an intermittent oxygen tank.

A RATIONAL APPROACH

We are taught to try to view people through a lens of compassion when observing questionable behaviors; to see things through their eyes. Take for instance a boss who is presenting your work as his own, making it look like you aren't contributing.

You may try a rational approach of speaking to him directly, especially if he is impeding your opportunities. That is a mature and sensible solution. But, with some people, a healthy adult approach doesn't work.

He may deflect, giving you some lame excuse on why he did what he did, but you know it won't make a difference. He will continue presenting your work as his own because he sees your work as the result of his brilliance in managing you.

Or, she may perceive an adult discussion as a challenge to her authority. She bellows and puffs up, telling you that the "accusation" of taking your idea is preposterous and that she has had that thought in her pocket for months. She wields her power over you, enjoying the rush of putting you in your place for even thinking of questioning her actions.

The real disgrace is that the idea stealers in both cases end up being rewarded. They get away with it. Sometimes there are enough people who complain to a higher up about the person's negative behaviors. But, the boss might be dysfunctional too. To avoid the conflict inherent in adult conversations, the idea stealer's dysfunctional boss coordinates a transfer to a different department for the offender. The boss has effectively kicked-the-can to someone else where the idea stealer does the same thing to other unwitting victims. The disease spreads.

These types of people are part of that 10 percent of dysfunctional individuals who cause problems within a company culture. These folks are peppered throughout all levels of an organization. And they're not going anywhere. They are a balanced, distributed part of a dysfunctional culture.

I call these dysfunctional and toxic people: Corporate Conformists.

WHAT IS A CORPORATE CONFORMIST?

A Corporate Conformist is a person who thrives in the status quo of a dysfunctional company culture for their selfish gain.

In a functional company, there are fewer pockets of Corporate Conformists and more Rebels like you.

In a dysfunctional or toxic environment, there are many more Corporate Conformists who aren't like you at all.

There are two types of Corporate Conformists:

1. Retired in Placers (RIPs)
2. Power Abusers

RETIRED IN PLACE (RIP)

I learned this term from an old school Westinghouse executive: RIPs = Retired in Placers.

RIPs can do nothing and rely on the power of inertia to reach their goals. They can let other departments cover the slack and capitalize on the annual incentive plans achieved by the company at large.

RIPs are the folks who take up space at the office. They accept promotions to critical positions of authority at the organization. Then they sit there. For years. They wait out vacancies until they are the only choice for another promotion. By that time, they have the confidence that they can handle the job because they have observed it for so long. What they don't have is any real passion for what they do.

RIPs evaluate work through a time and effort lens:

- Will this initiative increase the time I spend at work?

- Will this add more to my existing responsibilities?
- Can I stretch out my current project, so I don't have to work on this new initiative?

They are the people who use the full hour in a meeting thanks to their small talk in the first thirty minutes. Or, they schedule meetings for the sake of having meetings. That way, they have proof about why they can't take on new work—they are so busy! RIPs direct employees to solve minor, meaningless problems. They frustrate their teams with a general lack of opportunity to work on anything satisfying.

Kevin, a director of provider relations in a large health insurance company, explained his experiences with RIPs:

"Risk-averse or complacent management is a miserable situation for those that like to move the needle. Many of us like to see the advancement of our situations so we can progress our value faster. For those that strive for high achievement, having a manager that 'checks the boxes' is a terribly difficult situation."

An RIP will not be the one to pick up the ball and drive change. They never give concrete answers or make tough decisions. These are the people who wait for others to take the initiative. You hear things like "that's not my job" or "the business will have to make that decision."

Resistance to change is the hallmark of RIPs. RIPs subvert proposed changes by dragging their feet and not putting forth the effort. They say the right things to the higher-ups, but their behavior demonstrates a half-hearted attempt to embrace the change. RIPs know that by putting forth passive resistance to innovative ideas, the change makers will eventually give up.

For RIPs, not taking any action at all is a choice—a choice of inertia. A choice of maintaining the status quo.

Your ideas are hatched at the bottom of the food chain. This means for the idea to come to life, the RIP will have to elevate the idea to his boss. That has the potential to make him accountable for the result, which is an uncomfortable position for an RIP. Rebels like you are an overt threat to an RIP's personal inertia.

Sometimes they point fingers, saying that their "team," the minions, can't pull it off. Sometimes they use "bandwidth" as a reason, knowing that it isn't the case. Sometimes, they take an out of the blue, two-week vacation.

Take for instance, Jane. Jane made 150 phone calls during her eight-hour shift on her first day of her new job with a healthcare company. The next morning, her manager told her that she was making too many calls. She instructed Jane to make only thirty-five phone calls for the entire day.

> *"I knew I could make so many more calls, but she said that if I do more than thirty-five, I would make the rest of them look bad. I learned later that the average number of calls was thirty-five calls on an eight-hour shift. I could do that in forty-five minutes and take off the rest of the day!"*

Jane was blown away. She felt that her boss and peers were ripping off the company and their customers. Because they were. Jane's boss was an RIP, sandbagging the numbers to keep it easy-peasy in her department.

Emmanuel, a president of a Nigerian IT company, explained his experience with RIPs. *"There are those who want to do the 9-5 shift along the path of least resistance. They look for the safe harbor and drop anchor."*

RIPs are the water that puts out the fire of passion in Rebels like yourself. They've got no giddy-up. What's worse is when you work with an RIP, you find that they add time to all projects that survive their initial resistance.

The second type of Corporate Conformist is the Power Abuser. It is the Power Abusers that make your work life truly miserable.

POWER ABUSERS

Power Abusers want you to submit to their power. That's it. Their tactics differ, but it is all the same. Submit or else. They want to be in charge. They want you to obey. They want what they want. They have their plan, and you are going to help them get there.

The more power they get, the more they want, and if they aren't shown the respect that they think they deserve, you are singled out as enemy number one.

All the differing labels and dialects to "make people submit" make it harder to tackle power abuse. Whether it is mansplaining, bullying, discrimination, or harassment, it's all the same thing—power abuse. If we no longer had these disparate labels and simply called this power abuse, there might be a stronger voice in identifying and eliminating the behavior. Power abuse is when a person uses the power they have for their personal gain and to support their sense of entitlement.

Sexism, or racism, or discrimination is also power abuse. We will dive into this subject later in the book, but for now, just know that it is one person exerting power over another based on their sense of entitlement. This type of power abuse doesn't even require a person with positional power. Its ugly head can rear itself anywhere and at any time by anyone.

Name calling, singling out a person, excluding people on purpose—it's all power abuse. The intention is to make you feel bad, so you conform to Power Abusers' wishes and stay in your rightful place—which is beneath them.

Power Abusers aren't compensating because they lack self-esteem. Instead, they feel entitled because of their own perceived brilliance or birthright. They direct their anger at you when you don't meet their expectations of doing as they have commanded. You must submit or be destroyed. When good people fail to obey blindly, it does not fit into a Power Abuser's expectation of being faultless.

Ethics and morals don't enter the picture if they stand in the way of winning. If a toxic Power Abuser has to step on others' toes to get what they believe is theirs, they do. Profit and power trump ethics.

Power Abusers in seats of authority can yell, manipulate, and bully people with no fear of losing their job—providing they have increased their numbers or productivity over last year. When the numbers are there, their enabler bosses are placated.

On a business level, Power Abusers see through a selfish lens:

- How does this initiative benefit me? Does this work enhance my reputation? Does it get me a bigger bonus? A better title?
- What initiatives do I need to deploy to build my resume, and who do I need to use to get there? Who do I need to eliminate? Who are my enemies?
- Who do I want around me to make me look more potent than others?

What's worse is if you have a promising idea, and it is a game changer, Power Abusers internally fume. Power Abusers want to

stand out and dominate in front of their peers and senior leaders.*
A Power Abuser will kill your idea if it means that he is no longer
the smartest guy in the room. He can't have you stealing his
spotlight. Remember, when a Power Abuser has positional power
above you, it means that the threat of retaliation will always
be there.

Some power abuse is so subtle that it forces you to question
your own sanity. Its nasty intent is like a whisper. This type of
power abuse is easy to overlook, and if you aren't tuned in to it,
you'll miss it. Robert, a wealth manager at a global bank, said, *"It
was like catching smoke. I was unsuccessful in proving the bullying,
and the unhappy accuser eventually quit."*

Renee, a corporate lawyer, added, *"Bullying is not always so
obvious. The victim experiences it, but the alleged perpetrator is slick.
In one case, the claim was based on a sense of being cut off, ignored,
talked around, deliberately alienated by choice of topic in general
conversations—all of which proved extremely difficult to prove
but left the accusers in the same beaten condition as one who was
overtly bullied."*

Power Abusers will protect themselves at any cost, sacrificing
people for their political survival. Their behavior continues
unchecked, and once all is destroyed, they move onto the next
department or company. Orc style.

THE BALANCE OF CORPORATE CONFORMISTS

There are no consequences for the two types of Corporate
Conformists inside a dysfunctional company. It doesn't matter if

---

* Raven, B. (2008). The Bases of Power and the Power/Interaction. Analyses of
Social Issues and Public Policy, Vol. 8, No. 1, 1-22.

they ruin another person's health while they work there. It doesn't matter if they destroy the local economy with their bad decisions or lack of making a decision.

Corporate Conformists attract each other and insulate the dysfunction to sustain the inertia. There is an equilibrium between the two. A Power Abuser's behavior is tolerated by an RIP. Remember, RIPs don't want to change anything, so they just let the Power Abusers have their power and push the impossible demands on to you. RIPs wash away the sins of the Power Abusers, which maintains the dysfunction, which sustains the inertia.

YOUR BRIGHT IDEA IS TREATED AS A DEADLY VIRUS

So here you are, inside a sea of corporate conformity.

When you propose a solution, you believe your forward-thinking and ethical ideas will be embraced. But, when the idea is undeniably good, Corporate Conformists become twitchy.

Your novel solution exposes the issue that was either not noticed or purposely ignored by the Corporate Conformists. The change you propose forces Corporate Conformists to consider the problem differently.

It also creates an immediate dissonance with how your solution reflects upon their professional reputation. They see themselves as more relevant than you, more capable after all. If you were better than them, your title would reflect it.

Conformity is safe. Innovation takes guts. Their internal dialogue sends them into defense mode. This resistance results in their efforts to nix the idea before it can get off the ground. They say they want innovative solutions, when in fact what they want is the same thing that they have today: certainty inside of the conformity.

When great ideas are obvious and then shot down, our jaws hit the floor. Our colleagues say, "Welcome to the company," shaking their heads right along with us.

The same patterns of inertia continue. Equilibrium with corporate conformity is restored.

Most Rebels will press the issue, saying, "Hey, you don't understand. This idea is really good. Let me explain the benefits in a different way."

In a functional environment, this is a logical step. In a dysfunctional environment, you just put yourself square in a field of hidden dangers.

IT ISN'T YOU. IT'S THEM.

It isn't you. It is them. You have been drowning in the Corporate Conformist swamp of dysfunction. There are so many books out there that tell you that you need to focus on what you can do to remedy the situation. That you are responsible for "managing your manager." That you are the driver of your success. How can you be successful given these forces working against you?

The bottom line is this: Corporate Conformists don't think like you. What seems rational to you is an overt threat to how they want their work lives to be. When you have Corporate Conformists fighting to protect the status quo, your life as a Rebel is rough.

Because you don't think as they do, you end up feeling frustrated, stressed, angry, disappointed, and, worst of all, that your work has no meaning.

EXTERNAL FORCES VERSUS INTERNAL FORCES

Ok, so we trudged through some ugly stuff about work. It is important to know what you are up against, so you can reset your mind around what is versus what should be.

How a Corporate Conformist behaves is currently outside of your control. But your internal dialogue and behaviors at work are in your control. In a business relationship, it takes two to tango. You are a living, breathing part of the business ecosystem and can alter the status quo, if you know how.

But first, let's take a look at how you might be contributing to your own stress and how to fix it.

CHAPTER 3

Why You Are Frustrated
and What to Do About It

I INTERVIEWED HUNDREDS OF REBELS LIKE YOU FROM SIX continents to find out what drives them crazy at work and what they do to create their own success. Here are some of the main reasons that people are frustrated when they work with Corporate Conformists:

- Lack of Leadership
- Micromanagement
- Lack of Appreciation
- Lack of Communication
- Lack of Trust
- Lack of Respect

- Lack of Accountability
- Lack of Teamwork
- Lack of Direction
- Lack of Clarity About Responsibilities

There are other workplace stressors, but these are the type that has one common denominator. People. Specifically, the tensions between people.

Unexpressed feelings compound the powerlessness you experience when working with Corporate Conformists. You may not say a word, internalizing the negativity that festers inside of you.

You want to scream that Corporate Conformists are screwing everything up and that they are failing to meet your expectations of being a cooperative and productive professional. You can't bark at your boss, *"You were supposed to have this work done two weeks ago, Jimmy! Maybe we should take your phone away so you quit texting in meetings and focus on your job instead."*

The effort you expend to hide your emotions at work can deplete your energy in a matter of minutes. You fail to be true to yourself when you have to bury your thoughts and feelings to survive.

Emotions and feelings exist whether we like it or not. Suppressed emotions have physical manifestations, such as clenched teeth and increased heart rate. The negative energy you've absorbed from your environment spins around in your mind, growing in size and intensity like a hurricane increasing in strength.

If you can't express yourself at work and must bite your tongue, what do you do?

Some people handle stress in healthy ways—yoga, meditation, or talking with a friend or a counselor. But some of us lean toward the unhealthy outlets for an immediate fix. Do you know anyone who "emotionally overeats" or drinks to excess? How about any meds or recreational drugs? No judgment here. Everyone handles stress differently.

Your friends who work outside the office say, "Just quit!"

Yeah. Right.

Some people find new jobs easily, but other people can't leave their current role. Some people make the decision to stay and suffer because they have children in college, and the timing isn't right. Some people worry that the next place will be worse. Still others stay out of spite to police to the corruption, protecting their customers and their local economy. Other people genuinely love their work.

The bottom line is that there are Rebels who don't want a few bad apples to ruin what used to be a great place to work.

These are the real examples of why people stay in a dysfunctional environment. But in doing so, negative thoughts today layer on top of negative thoughts from the day before when you can't achieve the results you desire. This repetition exacerbates feelings of sadness, irritability, or even anger for those who feel that they have no hope.

WHY YOU ARE ACTUALLY FRUSTRATED AND WHAT TO DO ABOUT IT

To transform our mindset, we need to understand a simple concept about expectations and how they impact our feelings at work.

Feelings about neutral events vary from person to person based on their life experiences. Expectations are firm beliefs that something will happen or that someone will achieve something. Feelings are created by reactions to met, unmet, exceeded, and uncertain expectations:

- **Meeting expectations leads to neutral feelings.** Because you expect a certain outcome, you aren't phased when it happens as anticipated.
- **Unmet expectations lead to negative feelings.** You expected something to happen, but because it didn't, you feel sad, angry, disappointed, and frustrated.
- **Exceeded expectations lead to positive feelings.** You didn't expect a positive outcome, so you are surprised, happy, joyful, and/or excited.
- **Uncertain expectations lead to feelings of worry, doubt, and anxiety.** You aren't sure what to expect, so your mind takes you to the extremes of trying to predict what will happen. People like a definitive yes or no; right or wrong. Feeling uncertain about anything is, in my opinion, the worst feeling of all.

When your expectations at work are met or exceeded, your confidence and happiness grow. You have self-assurance that your work is valued, and you're also reassured of your ability to deliver. This sense of positivity is what emanates from confident people and draws other like-minded individuals into their orbit.

Negative feelings have the opposite effect. When your expectations are not met, your confidence shrinks. You don't think that your efforts will matter. You don't think that you can contribute toward a purposeful solution. You exude negative energy and self-doubt.

Feelings of uncertainty develop into feelings of anxiety that linger with us all day long. Uncertainty is what stresses us out the most, whether it be generated by a health issue, business outcome, or even a social situation. Why? Because we have no idea what to expect. Most people crave the expected, certainty, a roadmap, and instructions to make them feel secure.

WHAT ARE YOU FEELING AT WORK RIGHT NOW?

If you are happy and confident it is because your expectations are met or exceeded. You have self-assurance that your work is valued. Your positivity draws other like-minded individuals into your orbit.

If you feel stressed and frustrated, it is because your expectations are not met. Your confidence shrinks. You thought you knew what you were doing, or at a minimum, what was going on. Apparently, you didn't. You exude negative energy and self-doubt.

If you feel uncertain and anxious it is because you have no idea what to expect. Perhaps there are rumors about layoffs or about the retention of a valued customer. You radiate a vibe of worry and anxiety.

Expectations and feelings tie into self-esteem. Met or exceeded expectations lead to positive feelings, which lead to confidence. Unmet or uncertain expectations lead to negative feelings and less confidence.

Let's dig into this a bit more.

IMAGINE CLIMBING A LADDER

Imagine climbing a ladder that is leaning against a wall. Each rung of the ladder is an incremental step where you satisfy a small expectation of yourself. Each rung presents the choice of meeting that expectation or failing to meet that expectation. If you meet the expectation, you become more confident and take a step up the ladder toward confidence. If you fail to meet that expectation, you lose confidence and drop a rung.

When you are doing well at work, and everything is clicking, you are steadily climbing that confidence ladder. The climb is easy. You expect to be successful. You have a spring in your step.

When you are uncertain about what to do, you are in a holding pattern on a rung. You aren't sure what to expect. Your confidence neither grows, nor shrinks, but your anxiety is high.

But when you are not meeting expectations, you lose confidence and slide down that ladder. Sometimes a few rungs. You may have been given a goal and you failed to meet it. You are insufficient in your mind, and don't think that you can do anything to change the situation.

THIS ALL HAPPENS IN YOUR MIND

Confidence is built upon meeting and exceeding your own expectations of yourself. When you have proven to yourself that you can do something, you reinforce the expectation that you will succeed again. Confidence is what allows you to be resilient in the face of adversity. Because you believe in yourself, you know that there are workarounds to get up to the next rung. You might need to ask for help, but your belief in progressing upward never falters. In a functional company, you have people cheering you up that ladder.

When you are not confident, it is because you have experienced multiple failures. What you expected to do just didn't come to fruition. A lack of confidence results in people quitting before they even try. You have put forth a new expectation that you will not succeed at the same effort in the future. A lack of confidence creates a belief there is no way you can succeed, and you take a step back down the ladder. In a dysfunctional company, you have people blocking your path.

- *My boss is a micromanager—I must not be doing something right.*
- *I am confused about the direction on this—I must not be sharp enough to grasp what he means.*
- *I never get any feedback on my work—I don't know if I'm doing a good job or not.*

This is what it is like when you try and fail every day to be successful in a dysfunctional workplace. There is too much uncertainty to advance, and if you work with a boss who is power tripping or spinning their wheels, you assume it is your issue, and your confidence drops.

You lack hope that you can do anything to climb that ladder. You feel like you are deficient.

When you find that something is upsetting you, reflect on the situation. Were your expectations met or not met? How did that make you feel? Did your confidence go up or down?

When you find that something has delighted you, reflect on the situation. Were your expectations exceeded? How did your feelings change?

THE POWER OF EXPECTATIONS

There is incredible power in the knowledge of how expectations, feelings, and confidence work together because you can choose your feelings in advance.

People say that they need to have meaning in their work. It isn't about finding personal meaning in your work as much as it is to feel confident and capable that your behaviors produce an expected result. If you are confident, that means you are happy, which means you have met or exceeded your expectations.

Showing yourself that you *can* facilitates an empowering transformation. In doing so, you are claiming your sense of self-worth, purpose, and authenticity. You have met your expectations of who you are in the world. Your self-esteem is validated by how others respond to you.

The next time you set a goal, ask yourself, "Do you expect that you can do it?" The voice that answers will tell you if you will be successful or not. Asking if you *expect* to prompts a yes or no answer.

Then, you can ask yourself why. Stop and consider the reasons that you expect, or don't expect, to be successful and write them down.

Asking yourself if you expect to fulfill the goal leads you to identify the specific reasons you are blocked so you can get down to the nitty gritty of what needs to change. When you are in control of creating your own expectations, you have the opportunity to manage your feelings.

THE SECRET—DO YOU EXPECT TO?

In any situation, when you ask if you expect to do something, you have an opportunity to try, quit, or hang out on that ladder until you can advance again. You can stay right where you are until you decide.

When the answer is yes, and you do expect that you can do something, even if you failed before, you move into a place of confidence and commitment. You may realize that you need some coaching to be able to commit and fulfill your goal, but you still expect that you can do it.

When the answer is no, and you don't expect that you can do something, you move into a place of no confidence and negative feelings. But here is the secret. When you are finally ready to take on the challenge of the change, the reasons you listed for not expecting to do it are the exact behaviors that you will need to adjust should you want a different result.

Understanding expectations about work situations allows you to analyze a situation to see what you can change in the future. This control allows you to proactively manage your stress.

CHAPTER 4

You Aren't the Only One Climbing Ladders

When there is tension between you and an individual, you should ask yourself if your expectations were met or unmet. But then you need to ask yourself whether the other party's expectations were met or unmet, as well. You may be surprised when you find that you are the person who is indeed at fault. Did you communicate what you expected, or did you think that the other person could read your mind?

It is difficult to have a firm sense of what another person may be thinking at any given time. Consider the last argument you got into with someone. Was it because there was gap in communication based on each party's individual expectations? Chances are, a disparity in expectations had a lot to do with it.

THE EXPECTATIONS BOX IN A DYSFUNCTIONAL COMPANY

		OTHERS' EXPECTATIONS	
		You FAIL TO MEET others' expectations	You MEET others' expectations
PERSONAL EXPECTATIONS	You MEET your expectations — CONFIDENCE I EXPECT TO	**THE TRANSFORMATION** You feel hope in yourself They want you to submit	**THE REBEL SMUGGLER** You define your success They support me without knowing it
	You FAIL TO MEET your expectations — NO CONFIDENCE I DON'T EXPECT TO	**THE DOUBLE WHAMMY** You feel shame They humiliate you	**THE FOREHEAD SLAP** You feel anxiety They aren't paying attention

CONFIDENCE LADDER

We all work with people who have their own confidence ladders. Sometimes people will try to knock us down, or even off, our confidence ladder to maintain the expectations they have about themselves. They throw rocks of doubt at us, hoping that we will quit climbing. They diminish our confidence, which creates negative feelings.

When you marry your expectations of the need to create a new solution with a Corporate Conformist's expectations that the priority is to maintain the status quo, there are four potential outcomes, which, in general, can teach you a great deal about how you feel about your job.

These outcomes are:

- The Double Whammy
- The Forehead Slap
- The Transformation
- The Rebel Smuggler

THE DOUBLE WHAMMY

Let's assume your Corporate Conformist boss gives you an unreasonable goal. You try to pin him down to reach consensus on the deliverable, but he explodes and deflects saying he shouldn't have to tell you how to do your job.

You put forth your best effort building a PowerPoint, or working nights and weekends, to get him what you think he wants. The due date arrives, and you give him the presentation.

He approaches you, holding the PowerPoint, and in front of your colleagues says, "This isn't what I asked for."

This is the third time this month that this has happened. You have lost confidence in yourself to deliver anything of value, and you doubt your ability to do your job. Your boss has expressed his dissatisfaction openly. He has not offered any suggestions to make things better. You are uncertain about how to even remedy the situation. You are ashamed, humiliated, and have lost all hope of being successful in your role.

You don't expect to meet his expectations, and neither does he. You aren't good enough in your eyes or his. When you are ashamed, and your boss is publicly humiliating you, you've got yourself a "Double Whammy." Your spirit is crushed, and you feel sad and depressed.

Humiliation is created when you think someone else sees that you aren't good enough, or they openly tell you that you aren't. They expect you to fail. Humiliation pushes your internal shame button. You feel embarrassed because someone is intensifying your self-doubts with sentiments like, "There is no way you can do that," or, "You are kidding yourself."

That negative self-talk, combined with external humiliation, plays in a constant loop in your head, in some cases for years. In one tiny moment in time, this person impacted your identity so profoundly that you carry an imaginary boulder of shame on your shoulders, along with his boulder of humiliation.

Shame is felt internally. Humiliation is experienced externally. Both impact your confidence. Over time, shame and humiliation may impact your ability to try anything, causing you to fail to reach your full potential.

Your internal shame has already caused you to take a step back on the ladder, and a Power Abuser Corporate Conformist amplifies the situation with whispers or open declarations to take you down a notch. His public admonishments also send a message to others that they too must submit.

Margaret, a social worker, said, *"I was working with teenage boys at a residential facility, so they already had a negative attitude toward life. They were trouble makers, but they were smart, and they saw the flaws in the system and hated the place all the more. It was harder to support them and show that the world can be a safe, supportive place when their treatment facility did not hold to that value system."*

Experiencing a Double Whammy is awful. You feel like a loser, and you are made to feel like you are not good enough.

THE FOREHEAD SLAP

When Corporate Conformists are oblivious that something needs to change, and you know you could fix it if they let you, you are in the midst of the Forehead Slap.

Negative feelings arise when you are not meeting your expectations of what and how much you can contribute. This is especially true when others ignore either your talents or the need to solve obvious problems in the workplace.

It's as though you're holding a fire hose while watching a building go up in flames. You're waiting for permission to drench the fire, and the fire chief says, *"You are doing a great job. Just keep on holding that hose. No need to turn it on."*

Time ticks on. A Power Abuser may know what you have to offer but won't allow you to step up because doing so could mean a threat to his reputation or his initiatives. An RIP won't want to work on the problem because it costs him more time.

You try to climb a rung of the ladder, but he tells you that you aren't allowed to advance.

You have no confidence that the powers that be will wake up to see your value or what is needed for your organization to survive. You expect them to notice the obvious and do what is sensible in the situation, and they fail to meet your expectations time and again. This causes a harmful emotional strain that grows over time.

With zero control over the situation, you have unknowingly put yourself in a state of anxiety. You are worried about the uncertainty of "when" or "if" they will wake up to see the fire burning around them. You are convinced that you are powerless. The stress you feel is caused by their lack of acknowledgment that those problems even exist.

THE TRANSFORMATION

In the past two scenarios you have felt deficient, unable to turn around a negative situation, or both.

But you need to realize that the problem is not you—it's them, and it is the turning of the tide. You do not need to "fix" yourself. You are awakened and self-aware. You see that the leadership within your organization is dysfunctional. It is a wakeup call: You have to change your mindset to get any results.

Rebels like you can no longer participate in the dysfunction. You can no longer repress your get 'er done nature. You must hide your intellect, passion, and compassionate nature to appear as though you are drinking the company Kool-Aid. By hiding your nature and appearing like you have conformed, that you are part of the status quo, you are able to protect their job.

But with this awakening, you have transformed. You have decided that you will no longer allow Corporate Conformists to lead you around by the nose, making you feel inferior. You realize that they are the ones that need fixing. Your confidence rises.

This is a massive mental shift. This pivot elevates a person with no confidence to a new level of certainty. This is where people move from the point of *I don't expect that I can change anything*, to *I expect to change everything. Watch me.*

You must dig deep to talk yourself out of the perspective that you *can't* and bend it to the expectation you *can and will*. It is a conscious decision. You persevere until you have one success under your belt, and then you do it again by reaching for the next small win. Each successful attempt leads you to the point of knowing that you can. Not thinking—*knowing*.

Corporate Conformists see a change in you. They want to feel powerful and to make you submit. But you aren't resisting them. Now that you know the rules, you can play intelligently.

Empowerment is caused by you. But the change in your outlook, your perspective, and your energy is felt by them. Corporate Conformists feel they have exercised their power over you and won. They think you have submitted based on your purposeful behavior, which makes it appear as though you do as you are told.

It is akin to leaving a decoy on the confidence ladder. The Corporate Conformist fixates on the decoy while you keep climbing your ladder, notching off success after success. You haven't submitted at all. Your mind is more active than ever. When your leadership has either a flawed vision or no vision at all, you can choose to create your own.

You are persistent and tenacious. You try today, and the next day, and the day after that. There are always options around advancing an idea when your confidence is unshakable. You now see Corporate Conformists as static obstacles, and you smuggle your innovative ideas and projects around them.

You adopt the belief that the problem at hand isn't hopeless—that there is another way to solve it. The passion inside of you shines brighter than the dysfunction around you.

THE REBEL SMUGGLER

You have created your strategy inside of their game and are getting the results you seek. Each win builds your confidence. Confidence and results are generated and measured by you in your mind. When your tensions are minimized, ideas are able to move faster through the pipeline.

Banging your head up against the wall becomes a thing of the past. There is no structure of permanence. You have strategically maneuvered around the obstacles that Corporate Conformists have put in the way to hold you back, and you are no longer on their radar. They believe that you have submitted. They have no idea that they are the ones who have been led. By you, the Rebel, turned Smuggler.

You see everyone's confidence ladder. You see where they are gaining confidence, and where they have lost confidence and why. You see how some people are throwing rocks to maintain their "rightful" place above others. You see how others don't want to climb on their own and instead elect to ride the coattails those flying up the ladder.

In your professional environment, you now:

- Lead yourself
- Define and communicate your responsibilities
- Celebrate your accomplishments on your own
- Create expectations for yourself and others
- Demonstrate respect through accountability, meeting and exceeding expectations
- Become the example of being a great team player

Transforming into a Rebel Smuggler deserves its own chapter. So keep reading to learn more about these two empowering states of mind when working with others.

MANAGING EXPECTATIONS CREATES ACCOUNTABILITY AND BUILDS TRUST

When everyone's expectations are met, this builds something significant—trust. Accountability is the act of meeting expectations: yours and those of whom you interact with daily. Meeting expectations helps people build confidence in themselves and builds trust with others. When people are accountable to both their expectations and yours, everyone wins.

Be clear with others on what you expected to happen in the past and what you expect to happen moving forward. Take control of the negative feelings that make you emotionally sick.

If you are frustrated with someone right now, communicate what you expected to happen versus what did happen. Reset the conversation. Be explicit with your future expectations and listen carefully to theirs.

If a person fails to meet your expressed expectations again, then they have given you the gift of an observable pattern. Expect the pattern to continue. They will not be reliable, and you can design ways to ensure you get what you need without requiring them to change at all.

On top of that, when you meet or exceed expectations for you and for others, you create positive feelings. When a person has positive feelings, they are more confident, which not only creates a greater sense of trust but also makes them more likely to want to work with you. You make them feel good. They want to feel good. People are inclined to do what they enjoy first and procrastinate doing what they don't enjoy.

Your ideas will advance much faster with positive feelings associated with meeting or exceeding expectations.

EMOTIONALLY SENSITIVE PEOPLE

There are people who you work with who are more highly sensitive to criticism than others. They are impacted greatly when someone says something that knocks them down the confidence ladder because they might not have a baseline of confidence in themselves.

Things you say or do may never cross your mind as being harsh. But highly sensitive people respond differently to what seems to you to be a normal comment or situation. These people can be introverts or extroverts and are the ones who appear withdrawn or distracted in certain work situations.

Please be very careful with anything that might make someone feel humiliated when they are in a state of not having confidence in themselves. That is where you need to give them a hand up the confidence ladder. Granted, it is an external hand up. They will need to do the internal work of wanting to grab your hand. I don't have a surefire way to identify emotionally sensitive people. But please, use your intuition to help these folks build their confidence.

CHAPTER 5

Smugglers

With limited dysfunction, change driven by a Rebel is embraced. But if there is maximum dysfunction, then there is resistance to change, and that same Rebel turns into a Smuggler. If dysfunctional conditions didn't exist, there would be no need to smuggle change on the down low.

Not to be cliché, but an excellent example of the results of smuggling occurs when caterpillars evolve into butterflies. Caterpillars, like people, have an "immune system." The caterpillar immune system works to preserve "what is" until new butterfly systems are mature enough to function. The immune system seeks to maintain equilibrium—the status quo.

The company immune system is represented by Corporate Conformists. It is their job to maintain the stability of what is expected. Corporate Conformists who comprise the business immune system see Rebels as a threat to the status quo—which we are.

Corporate Conformists want the company to continue to exist as a caterpillar. It is what they know. You, however, want the company to evolve into a butterfly—it is what could be as a result of change.

If you're a Rebel who alters the equilibrium, you have a solid chance of being targeted as "bad" for the immune system. This is why you must mask your Rebel nature. If you don't, you will either be assimilated or destroyed.

Whether you are a Rebel in a functional company or a Smuggler in a dysfunctional company, you are the essential part of any transition. You are the catalyst that transforms the caterpillar into the butterfly. You disrupt the status quo and create opportunities for growth.

You are not the caterpillar nor the butterfly. *You are the magic that prompts the transition.*

Your creativity and need for results must have an outlet. It is your purpose. But when Corporate Conformists smother that creativity with conformity, that creative energy cannot be contained. The energy goes underground where change efforts are undetectable by Corporate Conformists.

CORPORATE IMMUNE SYSTEMS

A Smuggler's function is not to maintain or strengthen an organization as it is today. The aim of Smugglers and those who create change is not to destroy, but to fulfill a larger purpose, creative and otherwise, for the organization at large.

When the butterfly stretches its wings and starts flying, it still retains all the essential elements of the caterpillar. Similarly, companies that evolve in our changing world maintain the aspects of the existing business. It is the current business evolved into something better than before. Different, but better.

A caterpillar doesn't turn into a butterfly in an instant. Change uses the spark of just one Smuggler, who then finds others to create a network that is stronger than the Corporate Conformist network. The Smuggler network, when activated, creates a tipping point.

Smugglers are rarely, if ever, at the heads of corporations. That is because our function is to evolve and expand systems, not to maintain or strengthen the organization as it is.

Smuggling doesn't mean hiding something and giving it to someone who shouldn't have it. Smuggling is a philosophy. It is a way of thinking. It is an approach to change that requires patience, composure, intelligence, and rationality in the face of the inherent challenges of trying to alter the equilibrium.

Smuggling is about having confidence in the face of adversity. But it is also a belief that there is a better way—that you, through your efforts, can turn around the dysfunction and make things right.

We Smugglers wouldn't risk our necks to advance ideas just for the sake of doing so. We aren't altering our approach because we want to go underground or lose our jobs. We lead from the trenches to get our colleagues to willingly embrace change. Smuggling is neither done through PowerPoint nor email. We minimize fear and motivate others with conversations in-person every chance we get. A Smuggler's mission is to ignite movements without being politically "outed" and neutralized.

Smugglers are essential to transition. We are the people who lead Corporate Conformists from the status quo, through the hard part of the change, until we can build the team's confidence to continue on their own. We reassure Corporate Conformists that the change is safe, and that it is the right thing to do. That when the company evolves into one that is cooperative and sustainable, it will be to the benefit of employees and customers alike.

Smugglers open the eyes and stimulate the minds of people who didn't know they were blind and stagnant. You can identify Smugglers because they say things like:

- *Yes*
- *Let me see how I can accelerate this*
- *I will find resources*
- *We need to change things around here*
- *I will get this approved*
- *Why wouldn't we move fast on this*

It takes tremendous emotional and mental capacity to be a Smuggler. Our minion struggles don't get featured in magazines. But we Smugglers are the catalysts of change. We make change happen.

HOW SMUGGLERS SMUGGLE

Business as usual, or BAU, is the status quo. BAU is when all is comfortable and familiar. Relationships are stable, and everyone knows their job. Life is predictable.

Smugglers may not understand why they feel beaten every single day. The reason is that they are trying to get people not only to stop what they are doing but to run in a different direction.

The experience is akin to a private in the army telling the brass what needs to be done and then leading the charge.

This is when Smugglers must dig deep and find their grit. The transition from the status quo requires not just the initial step in the direction of the change but also the commitment to climb a steep slope. It takes an effort to persevere in climbing that slope from the starting line of business as usual.

Change requires a leap of faith. There are abundant uncertainties that might mean the bridge collapses under your feet or that the bridge is longer than you think. When a Smuggler proposes change, these are the types of thoughts that run through a person's mind:

- *Will the new changes require me to learn new skills?*
- *Will making this change make me look good or bad?*
- *Initiatives don't go anywhere anyhow, so why bother?*
- *What if I give it my all and I fail?*
- *How does this change my relationships at work?*
- *Will I have a job after these changes?*

Getting people to begin that uphill climb is hard to do, even when you are in a position of power. It is also hard for people to persevere until the change is adopted. This transition to change means that roles change, and nothing is clear-cut. Corporate Conformists see these factors as insurmountable obstacles.

Smugglers see the potential future as being better than the way things are today. The objective of smuggling is to advance an idea through the hazards of the status quo and a political machine created and sustained by Corporate Conformists. But the real value of Smugglers, who don't have the power or authority to create sweeping change, is their ability to convince people that the transitional part of the change is worth the risk.

When change is proposed, Smugglers make ideas popular and give unconditionally in an un-giving culture. We tell the right part of the story, to the right person, at the right time, and know how to explain the benefit to all, even the Corporate Conformists, so they want to back the idea.

People don't willingly change when the status quo is comfortable. That is why Smugglers use special techniques to seed doubt about the value in maintaining the existing way of doing business. The primary objective is to get people to move toward the bridge of change. (These techniques are explained in future chapters, so don't worry!)

The popularity of the idea takes nervous colleagues to the solid ground on the other side of the bridge with assurances that the new approach will reflect positively upon their reputation. With each passing day, the arduous work of the climb up the bridge builds trust in the team and in a person's confidence in their role. They can now form new routines and feel more stable with the increased certainty of what will happen. They know that what they are doing is contributing value. They have successfully crossed the "bridge of change" to the new status quo—the new equilibrium, which will exist until change is necessary for the next phase of growth.

Smugglers make others' ideas bigger and bolder. Smugglers understand a person's perspective and add to the value of their contribution, rather than point out why it won't work. Smugglers lift up colleagues along with them, helping people see their value and how their contributions made possible the end results. It is additive magic to improve the idea, not subtractive magic to take away from the concept's foundation. The focus is on the outcome of the work rather than what can benefit themselves personally.

SABOTAGE NONSENSE

There were friends of mine who cautioned me about writing this book. They said Smugglers sabotage the person in charge. My friends said that there are reasons people are in leadership positions and that I need to trust that they know what they are doing.

I disagree.

Smuggling is not sabotage. Sabotage is the deliberate effort to destroy something. Sabotage uses negative energy. There are individuals in the world who seek to ruin people's reputations. That is what Power Abusers do—destroy the enemy for their selfish gain. Smugglers add value for everyone in the mix.

UNLOCKING POTENTIAL

I was speaking with Joe Bautista, the chief creatologist for a multinational technology company. I explained the concept of Rebels who transition to become Smugglers. He understood what I meant immediately because he has been both a Rebel and a Smuggler, depending on the politics of the day.

Joe told me a story about a boss he had long ago. The boss told him, *"Joe you are like a free-range chicken. All of these company silos are like separate chicken coops, but you float between all of them and fit in and then bring them all together. I want you to unlock the value of our corporate silos."*

His boss got it. Joe wasn't wired like the other people in the company. He had the ability to see the potential across the entire organization and was empowered to bring it all together to create great success for the company.

He rose through the ranks to become one of the best innovators in the business, creating opportunities that others did not see. Some people viewed him as a valued Rebel. Others saw him as another conformist, when, in reality, he was simply smuggling.

That is the value of Smugglers. Smugglers know intuitively how to unlock the value of an idea by convincing people to come together, building their collective confidence so that they can achieve their goals. Smugglers see the opportunity with crystal clarity. The problem is that others inside the corporate machine don't think like "free-range chickens." They think the only version of the world that matters is the one that exists within their own chicken coop!

YOU ARE NOT ALONE

Smugglers realize that our thoughts often diverge from business as usual. It is why, if we voice our ideas overtly, we become radioactive to those who want to remain conformists. But, it is also how we attract other Smugglers.

When you find a Smuggler, and then find another, you create a network of people that get things done. Smugglers activate and empower other Smugglers throughout the organization. We aren't always in the same company or even the same country. While Smugglers appear across many socioeconomic workplaces, there is one global smuggling tribe.

We Smugglers recognize each other by our collaborative nature. Titles are irrelevant. David, a salesperson from the beverage industry, said, *"We are a team. We share our knowledge and ideas even though we work in different departments. We are always encouraging each other."*

When you meet a person who is aware that they can't achieve

anything, they are stressed and feel like they are the ones who are crazy and doing something wrong. When they meet you and sense that you are different, they are usually overwhelmed and grateful that they found you. You can communicate that you understand the struggle, and you can reassure that person that they no longer have to battle alone. You can almost hear their sigh of relief. You have given them hope.

THE TIPPING POINT

It is vital for you to create a coherent network of other Smugglers to ensure that you are not lonely in your view of the world. Smugglers believe change is possible once they hear success stories from other Smugglers in and out of the company.

Smugglers that link with other Smugglers create a movement. Movements are the force that changes the inertia. Invisible smuggling networks run like rivers throughout the world, allowing the flow of great ideas and fresh knowledge into the collective consciousness. Smugglers seek these inconspicuous channels as they function as a team of like-minded people who believe there is a better way.

Ironically, the most significant success for a Smuggler happens when someone else takes credit and requests a bigger budget to deploy the idea. There is no bigger win for a Smuggler than the acknowledgment that their concept is outstanding. That thrill comes in the form of others buzzing about the potential of the idea, not knowing that the Smuggler drove the idea from the bottom of the food chain.

We rejoice when minds convert, which happens at a snail's pace. Our small victories, when they come, are celebrated on the down low, inside the hidden Smuggler network. That is when we kick back, smoke a proverbial cigar with our small squad of disruptors, and wait for the next battle to begin.

Smugglers create movements. One mind at a time.

CHAPTER 6

How to Increase
Your Business Value

PEOPLE WILL ALTER THEIR BEHAVIORS IF THERE IS ENOUGH VALUE. Your challenge, regardless of your job title, is to get people to change their behavior voluntarily in exchange for the value you provide them.

Smugglers need to ask, "What behavior do I want to change?" before brainstorming any solution to be launched inside or outside of the company. This is what sets Smuggler solutions ahead of Corporate Conformist solutions.

Begin by focusing on the current behaviors of your end users or internal stakeholders. How does your product, idea, or service make a person want to stop what they do today, to switch to your proposed idea?

Consider the behaviors involved in mopping a floor.

I have memories of filling the bucket with soapy water and lugging it around the house. The smell of dirty water was always overwhelming as I would wring out the mop. The end of the mopping process was no better, because I would end up splashing dirty water on my clothes when pouring it down the drain.

I didn't enjoy the experience of mopping a floor. But these were the behaviors I demonstrated if I wanted a clean floor.

Swiffer wanted to create a product that would transform my experience. They wanted to shift my spend from buying other companies' mops and buckets, to buying Swiffer products. To do that, they needed to provide greater value than the process I used to get clean floors with the mop and bucket.

Swiffer's invention of a disposable springtime fresh scented "rag" on the end of a pole took the ick out of cleaning a floor. It didn't require me to deal with gallons of water or wringing out dirty water in my hands. On top of that, I could "mop" my floor with a Swiffer within a matter of seconds. All I had to do was pop a disposable pad on the end of a Swiffer. I could see the result of my efforts almost immediately which were just as good as mopping.

I was already exhibiting the purchasing behavior of buying buckets and mops. But Swiffer shifted my spend and behavior to a new way of mopping my floor by creating greater value for me to get to the result I desired—a clean floor. I will never use a mop and bucket again.

Thinking through the "customer experience" isn't just for customers. Smugglers have to consider the behavior changes necessary for the internal stakeholders of the company to ensure that the project comes to life. We must consider the behavior changes required throughout the entire stakeholder path necessary to create and sustain the idea—including the behavior of your leaders.

WE AREN'T AS COOL AS WE THINK WE ARE

The needs of humankind haven't changed in thousands of years. Whether it is how to grow food and transport it, finding places to live, staying healthy, communicating with each other, entertaining ourselves, or drawing attention to ourselves to accentuate our assets, man has had the same elemental needs since the beginning of civilization.

Humanity has always endeavored to create innovative solutions to these needs. A Smuggler's true north is creating value in five core areas which define the purpose of the solution and prompt behavior change.

Here are the essential human motivators that all new ideas and projects must impact to create behavior change. These motivators are represented by the acronym FIRST.

- Fun
- Identity
- Resources
- Symptom avoidance
- Time

When you are trying to change a person's behavior, you are actually solving for ways to improve on their FIRSTs.

F—FUN

You may change your behavior for the opportunity to do something fun, or, you may change your behavior to get out of doing something that isn't fun at all.

Fun in ancient times might have meant playing a game of

chance in person with friends. Fun today might mean playing Call of Duty remotely with friends. Incremental improvements in technology have removed the need to be physically close to friends to have fun. You don't have to be in the same room anymore to engage with others and take part in an enjoyable activity. But, fun is still a motivator for behavior change. That is why gamification has entered the business world—to make things fun, and to get you to change behavior in order to engage more closely with the brand.

It can also mean not having fun. If something isn't fun, then you avoid it. No offense to my biking friends but pedaling anywhere to me is just the worst thing in the world. I remember riding a bike through the tulip fields of Holland with my cousin while the tulips were in full bloom. I had a vision in my mind of how this experience would feel before we began. It would be like we were in a travel magazine, smiling as we saw the beautiful colors, pedaling along in the cool spring air.

Yeah. It wasn't like that at all.

We started, and within the first ten minutes I was ready to toss that bike into the sea of color and walk back to the car. The saddle was hard, my wrists hurt, and frankly, I was out of shape. She kept telling me it wasn't that much farther, which was a total lie. We went eighteen miles.

I couldn't walk comfortably for days. My wrists required some Dutch form of Advil for the rest of my vacation. Suffice it to say, it was not fun.

It changed my behavior. I will never, ever get on a bike again.

I—IDENTITY

You will modify your behavior if it promotes your identity, or if it goes against your identity. How you dress, how you behave, and how you think are all ways to showcase who you are, and who you are not, to the world.

In American culture, you might want people to think of you as an attractive woman based on the standards set in the latest fashion magazines. Your behaviors of going to the tanning salon, the beauty salon, and the nail salon support your identity of having "the look" of a model.

Another example is if you are a bank teller but are a comic book fanatic and attend Comic-Cons all around the country. Your behavior supports your identity, and you are always delighted when people compliment you on your handmade Ghostbuster proton pack.

If the attractive woman is given free tickets to the Comic-Con, but she doesn't believe that her "tribe" of fashion models would hang out with comic book aficionados, she may avoid attending the Comic-Con.

People modify their behaviors to support their self-identity.

R—RESOURCES

You will modify your behavior as it relates to resources. Resources can be money, or other types of units of value.

For instance, twelve thousand years ago you had to hunt or gather your food. Now we have grocery stores supplied by megafarms.

Megafarms created efficiencies in production (saving resources) as well as generating greater yields of food (increasing resources) using technically advanced production methods. Both farmers and consumers alike altered their behaviors to realize these resource saves and gains.

Another example of resources impacting behavior change is as simple as taking another job for higher pay. You had to change your behavior to send out resumes, interview for the position, and drive to a new job location to increase your resources (pay).

S—SYMPTOM AVOIDANCE

Symptom avoidance is a strong motivator for behavior change. For instance, diabetics who watch their sugar intake may restrict their diet because they don't want the symptoms of diabetes to impact their day-to-day life.

If you are healthy, you feel no need to change your behavior. But, if you are sick, your entire world is impacted. You are motivated to change your behavior to get out of feeling crappy or to even cheat death. Whether it is a witch doctor offering you poultices or your doctor investigating pharmacogenomics, you are motivated to keep the symptoms of sickness away however you can.

I've gotten some pushback that some people just want to be healthy, and their behaviors have nothing to do with symptom avoidance. For instance, the person who wants to be a size x. He alters his behavior and meditates to manage stress, walks five miles a day, and eats a balanced diet. Why does that person want to be healthy? In most cases, shrinking to a size x has to do with identity, not symptom avoidance.

T—TIME

Saving a person time is one of the biggies. Enabling an army to move swiftly in Spartan times meant that you got to get those troops from point A to B on foot. Today we transfer armies from point A to B on planes. We are motivated to save time, whether it is to get to our vacation destination faster or to maneuver troops to protect people.

Time savings is already a big focus for companies, but time is also a valuable behavior changing tool when working with internal stakeholders at your company. If you can save them time, they are more than happy to find other things to do.

FIRST COMES FIRST

A person willingly embraces change in exchange for these FIRSTs, providing there is enough value for the change. For instance, you may not change your commute to work if an alternate path saves you three minutes. But if it saves you twenty minutes, then you are more likely to change your behavior. The value to a single FIRST is relative.

The more FIRSTs you have, the better the chance for a behavior change.

Inventions like the iPhone are disruptive, yet I'm not sure folks realize that the disruption is behavior change. The iPhone changed various facets of human behavior, not just the way we use cell phones. It eliminated the behaviors of carrying a paper calendar, using a paper map, asking directions, wearing a watch, or carrying a camera.

The device covers every aspect of FIRST.

- Fun—The iPhone offers games and the ability to play videos and much more.
- Identity—The iPhone makes me look cool.
- Resources—The iPhone saves me money on buying all the other items.
- Symptom Avoidance—The iPhone allows me to talk to a doctor on my phone.
- Time—The iPhone save me time because information is at my fingertips.

NEEDS VERSUS BEHAVIOR CHANGE

The most dangerous and vital aspect of a Smuggler's work is shining light on the real problem. But the problem isn't what most business teams would think. The real problem is that companies launch solutions that fail to account for why a person would change their behavior to buy their product. They use the word "need." It isn't about need. It's about hitting a person's motivators for behavior change.

If your solutions are not revolving around these human motivators for your customers and your stakeholder chain, then your product or project will not get the traction you desire. But if your ideas do cater these motivators, especially if you can tailor a solution that fits every category of FIRST, you are on the road to disruption, which means the disruption in people's behaviors who engage with your products.

Do you have to shine a spotlight on the real problem—the need to focus on behavior change versus bells and whistles—in a way that doesn't tick off your Corporate Conformist? You bet.

But if the Corporate Conformists don't want to hear it, and

tell you to generate revenue no matter what, you need to put forth your best effort to create an idea that will focus on the FIRSTs for your customers and internal stakeholders.

A Smuggler may have a cure for cancer but knows that he must focus on hurdle number one—how does this new idea satisfy the FIRSTs for your boss? How about your marketing manager, sales director, and operations VP? What about vendors?

How does your project save them, personally, time and resources? How does your work impact their reputation? How does your initiative engage them to the point where they are having fun participating?

Don't begin an initiative without pinpointing the precise motivators and expectations of those you work with. Your first objective is to lower their resistance and change their behavior so that they're able to get on board with your idea.

SMUGGLERS CREATE THINGS THAT MATTER IN THE BIGGER PICTURE

A challenge was issued by Ford Motor Company to their suppliers. One of the suppliers passed along the challenge to its leadership team. However, Andrew's manager said, *"No way are we working on someone else's problem."*

Andrew realized the opportunity in the bigger picture, which was to exceed Ford's expectations. Doing so would create a deeper relationship, resulting in Andrew's company selling more to them. If his company could solve the problem for Ford, they would be building incredible value solidifying them as a customer. Not to mention that Andrew craved the thrill of working on a challenging puzzle in addition to his regular work.

"Ford tasked all of its suppliers to reduce insertion force on overhead system fasteners. The official company line was 'we're not working on that.' So, no one in the company put forth any effort on it.

I thought we could do it. So, I started doing some digging around and found an old alternative fastener design. Through some CAD design and FEA simulation I had 'snuck in,' I came up with yet a new alteration of that design. But there was no budget to prototype this thing and prove it out.

So, I found a naive Product Manager and told him we could have this thing ready for his project in just six months. It was just a little white fib, but he believed it and I wrangled some budget out of him to get a prototype tool built and then proceeded to test the thing.

Sometime later I left the company but learned that because of my 'skunkworks' demonstration project and how well it had worked, they decided to commission it as a real project and take it to market. Which they did, with great accolades from Ford. So, I like to think the 'beg, borrow, or steal' approach I used, including 'enhancing' the truth to do so, was as close to an unofficial, unsanctioned 'skunkworks' as I could get. I didn't know what else to call it. I suppose I was getting the innovation out, for the benefit of all. For me, I've always enjoyed doing these secret, undercover, skunkworks projects. It's a part of my weird DNA."

The manager was a Corporate Conformist who failed to work on a problem that would not only benefit Ford but the industry at large. Andrew saw the more significant potential and solved the problem on the lowdown by taking incremental steps outside of his department and focusing on the product manager's FIRSTs to smuggle the idea to life.

Andrew saw the challenge as a *fun* puzzle to solve that benefited the reputation (*identity*) of his department, the product manager, the company, and its customer, Ford. He told a fib about the six-month window, which was the *time* hook needed to get the product manager on board. He increased the *resources* (dollars) for the company with a new product. I'm stretching the limit on using *symptom avoidance* here, but let's just say when you are happy, you aren't stressed.

CHAPTER 7

Winners and Losers

THE I IN FIRST IS IDENTITY. IDENTITY IS A CRITICAL COMPONENT in thinking about how to engage people in corporate America. It deserves its own chapter because understanding a person's identity will help you the most, in your professional and personal life.

THE ARTIST AND THE HUNTER

Imagine that I have a friend named Pradeep who is a world traveler and an artist.

If I bought Pradeep a painting while traveling in Nepal, he would probably see it as a gesture of my respecting his identity and be delighted. I honor him as someone who is creative and superb at his craft by bringing him a gift from a foreign culture, based on his passion for brush types and pigments.

I would explain the nuance of the colors and paint strokes, helping him to see the time and skill it took to create the painting. By speaking in his language (jargon), I would create within him warm feelings for my tacit understanding of what he values. He sees his own identity reflected by me, as well as the gift. Recognizing a person's identity, and respecting that core, is what builds trust.

Imagine that I have another friend named Dennis. Dennis is a hunter in Western Pennsylvania and prefers hunting deer over other wildlife.

If I bought Dennis the same painting, he would probably look at it with a puzzled expression on his face. The delicate strokes and subject image would have no meaning to him and would be opposite of what he would expect, given his self-identity. He wouldn't even know the importance of the words I use to describe it.

But, if I handed him a long-range hunter's dream, a Deer Slayer III, and talked about the specs in detail, he might just love me forever. I am honoring his core identity.

A PERSON'S NUMBER ONE MOTIVATOR

Dale Carnegie said, *"A person's name is to him or her the sweetest and most important sound in any language."* I think that is only part of the puzzle. What is more important to a person is what that name represents—a person's identity as a whole. Their name, their style, their intellect, their speech, and the groups they affiliate with are all pieces that blend to form a person's authentic nature. After all, it takes time to try on many identities until you find one that resonates with who you truly believe yourself to be.

A person's identity is sacred to them. It is their most precious belief. In the process of identification, people expose not only who they are but also how they expect you to respect them. They also reveal their vulnerabilities. A statement for or against anyone's central identity is a motivator for change.

Neutral input, whether it is a conversation, a gift, or a headline in the news, either supports or detracts from a person's identity.

What people may not know is that a person's main identity is also their Achilles' heel. People will go to great lengths to defend the elements that make up their identity. Criticism about how someone views themselves can create impassioned feelings, including sadness, anger, and frustration. People might get into a fist fight over criticism about their identity, deny the reality of the truth, or decide to avoid people for fear of a negative reflection on their identity.

QUEST

To change a person's behavior, you must know how they view their identity. You then either support that identity or you create cognitive dissonance around that status. People change their behavior when their identities are challenged.

I was in my car listening to the radio show Fresh Air. Terry Gross was interviewing Jonathan Olshefski, who created the documentary Quest. The movie explored the lives of the working-class and poor African-American neighborhoods of north Philadelphia. The story centered around a man, Quest, who opened his home to allow kids and adults in the neighborhood to record their music in a safe space. Quest (Christopher Rainey) also participated in the interview. I cite his story as a way to understand the power that identity has on a person:

> *"I had two bad years of angel dust. I was smoking angel dust for two years. This was in the early '90s—'91, '92. It was a rough time in my life also. You know, actually I was going through a bad breakup and, you know, I was confused and hanging around with the wrong people. So, you know, it really—it took me two years. And what made me quit really—reality was a kid walked up to me that I knew. And I spoke to him. I was like, hey, what's going on? And he was like, 'Get out my face. I don't mess with you anymore. You get high. You ain't nobody to me.' And that hurt me. It broke me because I was so used to being respected by everybody in the neighborhood.*
>
> *When this young kid said that to me, it literally changed my life. I just literally stopped that day. I called my brother J.C. and I said, J.C., I don't want to get high anymore. What should I do? He sent a cab for me and brought me up to his house and I just hung out with him for, like, six months, and, you know, that was the end of it. I got better."**

I am so happy that Quest had such a high expectation of himself—he expected to be respected by his community. He knew he was worthy of being a role model. The kid didn't have the same opinion. The child reflected a negative image of his

---

* Gross, T. (2017, December 20). A Filmmaker's Quest for a Quiet Family Portrait is Pierced by Unforeseen Trauma. Retrieved from NPR: https://www.npr. org/2017/12/20/572238985/a-filmmakers-quest-for-a-quiet-family-portrait-is-pierced-by-unforeseen-trauma

identity, which motivated him to change his behavior. Quest believed he was better than the kid's perspective of who he was. Quest believed that yes, he was a role model, no matter what the boy thought of him at that moment.

To create change, you have to move a person to a position where the existing situation does not tie to their sense of identity. You tap on this point, from different angles, until they understand that for themselves. You create a crisis by demonstrating how the headline is indeed in direct conflict about who they think they are. When a person's internal lightbulb goes off, and they realize that their old way of thinking is wrong, they search for solutions on their own.

Remember, not everyone is starting from the same place of knowledge that you are. You must make them care about the problem and how it reflects on their identity to get to the crisis point where they seek out fresh solutions. There is no solution considered until there is a crisis with a person's identity. Patience is essential.

HOW TO PINPOINT IDENTITY

People reveal their identity with answers they give you in casual conversation. You, of course, can prompt their answers with questions about what they do on the weekend, or what life was like when they were growing up. Listen for the following clues:

- How I describe myself (I'm a manager, I'm a parent, I'm a cross-fitter, etc.)
- Things I have (I have a boat, I have an apartment in the city, a dog, etc.)

- Things I like to do outside of the office (I hike, I golf, I shop, etc.)
- I can't stand (Trump, Hillary, The Dallas Cowboys, liars, etc.)
- I remember in my younger days… (going on a family vacation, having nothing at all because we were poor, playing football in the yard, etc.)

Pay close attention so you don't ever hurt their feelings by saying something that insults this ultra-sensitive part of their psyche. For instance, if I am talking with Dennis and I say, "I don't understand how anyone can murder innocent animals," Dennis might stiffen. He does not see himself as a murderer. Quite the contrary. He sees himself as a compassionate hunter who prevents starvation of deer through hunting. He eats what he hunts, just like his family has done at camp since he was a child.

Do your interactions with people at work respect their identity? Are your "gifts" to your boss appropriate in supporting the way he sees himself, or is your initiative presented like artwork for a hunter?

GROUP IDENTITY

A person is born into a group—their family, or those who act as their family. The family shapes a child's identity and teaches what is valued and what is not in the group through words and behaviors.

Points of view on sexism, racism, and greed are seeded, contained, and nurtured inside of these groups, no different than positive qualities such as how to cooperate, care, give, and love.

The group's identity shapes the child's identity. None of this has to do with intelligence, ambition, or conscious decisions that the child has made. It simply is. As a result, this child forms an identity about himself or herself.

All the world's greatest thinkers learned from others in their communities, their groups. We process information through this point of view.

As people age, they get to choose the groups that reflect their identity to the world. For instance, a group identity that someone might want to "wear" might center around being an outdoorsman, or a dancer, or a powerful businessman.

All groups have identifying characteristics, such as physical attributes (hairstyles, grooming, fashion), possessions (cars, toys, jewelry), manners of speech, and generally, their behaviors in how they interact with the world. It is the culture defined by the group. When you are part of a group, you conform to your group's characteristics. The group reflects the aspect or aspects of your identity that you have consciously chosen.

Belonging to a group is the warm blanket that wraps itself around your precious identity—your authentic self. But, it isn't enough to just belong to a group. Once a person is accepted into a group and conforms to the rules, he craves the recognition of his efforts to contribute to the group.

We measure ourselves against others in the group. Measurement helps us understand if we are a "winner" or a "loser" compared to other people. Even product promotions are designed to play upon this psychology. Belong to this "group," and these "trophies" represent your membership. Are products marketed to make you feel that you are a loser if you don't have that particular brand, or are they marketed to make you feel that you are a winner because you do? Does possessing those cars, handbags, or toys represent your status as a member? This is why awards and other recognitions work. They validate the fact that you belong, as well as how you rank within a given group.

Validation also comes in the form of the behaviors of the members of the group—how they treat you, how they include you, and how they express the value of your contribution—all proving that you belong. Ideally, these behaviors will meet your expectations about how your central identity is received and respected, building your self-esteem and creating positive feelings of being a member to the group.

If we have decided that we want to be a part of a group, it is because we assume that its members are "better" in some way and will lift us to their level of awesomeness. We hear their words, view them admiringly, and believe what they say about the merits of group membership. Groups can take the form of a company, a university, a fan club, an ethnic group, a political group, or even a company silo.

AMERICAN COMPETITIVE MINDSET —WINNERS AND LOSERS

Americans value competition. We believe it will bring out our ingenuity and the best qualities in us—that by facing what seems to be insurmountable odds, our competitive spirit will allow us to persevere.

In my opinion, American culture used to be about good sportsmanship—two equally skilled players having a fun and competitive game to make things interesting. One person might win one day, another the next. There was mutual respect and politeness demonstrated for each person's best effort and play honestly by the rules.

But the pursuit of dollars has transformed how America pursues goals. Company profits and its reward systems drive employee behavior. A focus on the bottom line has replaced our creativity and curiosity in working on transformative work unless the profit margins are high enough. Decisions are made through a winning lens, a profit-at-all-cost lens, versus building products of value to customers and society at large. A profit-at-all-cost America to me feels like Disney telling Mozart to alter his music to sound a bit more like "Bibbidi-Bobbidi-Boo."

This isn't the competitive spirit that made America great. This isn't the freedom to explore the boundaries of our capabilities. Profit at all cost is an anchor restricting exploration, especially when that exploration is a threat to the status quo. Instead, profit at all cost is what sustains the status quo.

In today's cutthroat, competitive culture, second is first loser. With a competition mindset, a person's sense of self-worth is measured against other people. Ambition is rewarded by the public recognition of being a winner. A winner is "more powerful" than the loser.

The more a person competes, the more they must feed the beast to feel good about themselves. They have to find the next competition. It isn't enough to win. Competitive people must dominate.* If you think about it, you can't have power over another without competition.

It doesn't matter if a person enjoys the "game" or not. A person with a competition mindset needs the fix of competition—the fix of winning. Serious competitors seek to be better than the other guy. People use money, power, reputation, possessions, or other measurements to showcase their status in their designated groups.

---

* Fowler, T. (2015, January 19). High School Basketball Coach Suspended After His Team Crushes Another 161-2. Retrieved from People: http://people.com/celebrity/high-school-basketball-coach-suspended-after-his-team-crushes-another-161-2/

Competition is a zero-sum game—one person's gain is the other's loss. One person is a winner, and one person is a loser. For those of us who have been burned by the person seeking to win no matter what, we know that competition has the power to break trust and create resentment. *I didn't do it. He did. I'm not the loser.*

Did you know that many people don't compete to be a winner? Rather, they compete to not feel like a loser. Winning is just one side of the coin. Insecurity is also taught by the competition mindset. If someone else beats me and wins, that makes me a loser—and there is shame affiliated with being a loser.

Losses are personal. In a competitor's mind, being a winner is part of their identity. Members are the first to defend any contrary views against their group. But, should they lose to you, someone they think as "less than" them, a situation has been created that is in direct conflict with how they view themselves. You aren't a rival. You are now an enemy.

GROUPS, IDENTITY, AND THE AMERICAN COMPETITIVE CULTURE

When I address winners and losers, I do not mean winning and losing as it relates to sport, as in a quantitative measurement. Instead, the definition is a qualitative assessment, meaning, "I am better than you. I am a winner. You are beneath me. You are a loser."

When you have a group who believes that they are inherently winners, the competitive culture ensures that its members protect their group. Its members are the front-line defense safeguarding the reputation of the group as a whole. They are the first to attack when they sense any threat to the status of being the winning group.

Rick, from a large consulting firm, was pushing for the opportunity to become a partner. He realized he was just as good as the rest of them. He had proposed an aggressive revenue opportunity and said, *"If I make the goals, I want to be named partner."* His bosses didn't think he would deliver, so they agreed to his terms. Then they set him up to fail by continually adding more deliverables to the project, so they could blame him for being deficient and withhold the partnership.

He learned that one particular person was seeding doubt among the other partners, presenting Rick as *"just not ready for the job."* Rick was inferior in his eyes, and he worked on others in his elite partner group to make sure they saw Rick the same way. He used language and other gaslighting tactics to make him feel like he wasn't working hard enough.

It wasn't enough to accomplish the goals. Rick also needed to lower the resistance that this man was fortifying by spreading the word that he was "less than." Rick needed to smuggle himself in. He needed to penetrate the force field between his current group and the partner group.

Rick knew it wasn't enough for him to do it alone. He needed to find fellow Smugglers in the "winner" group to pull him into their circle, despite this man's attempts to block him. They were willing to run a block for him while he chipped away at the unreasonable goals.

He blew the goals out of the water and was eventually accepted as part of the "winner" group. He didn't have the full support of the fearful partner, which was okay. The man accepted that Rick was in the winner group. He wasn't happy about it but was able to lick his wounds by viewing Rick as low on the totem pole, still way beneath him in his eyes.

The people like this guy who are "protecting" the group from outsiders are in fact protecting their own precious identity. This man didn't like Rick for whatever personal reason. He felt that he was not equal to him and didn't want Rick to stand next to him, lest people think he was like Rick. He saw affiliation with Rick as lowering his value to those who view his group the same way as he does.

When a person's identity is challenged, they dig in to defend themselves. They can't personally be wrong lest they're forced to re-examine their identity, which they were convinced was rock solid. So, they defend the virtues of the group at large to avoid having to defend their personal perspective.

BEHAVIOR TO AVOID FEELING LIKE A LOSER

If a person's self-identity does not reflect what they expect of themselves, and how they want to be recognized by their group, they work longer hours, chase the next promotion, and don't find much time to reflect on why they are running so hard. They work hard every day to support the opinion they have of themselves. It's all to experience the feelings of being a "winner" because they can't see themselves as a loser.

If I see myself as a Wall Street financier but I drive a Kia, I may avoid picking up my boss for dinner and just meet him there. A winner, after all, would drive a Mercedes. I would not be reflecting the identity that represents the Wall Street group, and as he is part of the group, he would think I'm a loser.

DESPERATION TO BE A WINNER

Unethical actions don't just happen in one day. Morality and ethics erode a little bit each time a person chooses the low road. When a selfish person doesn't have the things that the "winners" have, that person may take unethical action, cutting corners to get to where they want to be. Greed warps ethics and people may seek fast and easy ways to become a "winner."

Selfish "winners" cut corners to get what they want, and they alter their behavior to avoid being caught. When greedy people get away with more, they then take a little more still, which gives them a false sense of security. Corruption lures people step-by-step into a downward spiral until they are in over their heads.

Nathan, a project manager, said, *"If you are on the edge of compromising ethics, those are not boundaries I want to be close to. Those folks are desperate, lack perspective, and are focused solely on personal benefit."*

MIXING GROUPS

The bottom line about racism, sexism, idea-ism, and elite-ism is that the dominant group considers themselves to be "winners." Their identity of being a winner prevents any "mingling" with those they consider to be losers—those "beneath" them who are of a different race, ethnicity, or gender, or a person with a "lower" department or title. (Think corporate silos.) It is competitive mindset group-ism, working hard to show that *my group is better than yours.*

Each "loser" like you who successfully joins the "winners" alters the power balance. Altering anything is change. But an uncertain power balance creates the most unsettling feelings of all—especially for people who are trying to protect their group and their own identity.

Take for instance an all-male executive team comprised

of Corporate Conformists. Adding a woman, who is not representative of the "winning" attributes of the group, means that they are no longer a true winner. A true winner would be top dog in the male group that exists. She is changing the power balance and possibly their own ranking inside of the group.

When these Corporate Conformists want to maintain what is, they may lock heads with this outsider—the woman. They may not include her in decision making or events. They need to believe that the men's group are the winners, and she is an anomaly to satisfy "diversity efforts" to maintain their self-identity of being a true winner. In these Corporate Conformists' minds, she is still less than them, and the way they treat her will reflect that perception.

If you are the woman in that situation and you successfully penetrate this group's force field, it can feel overwhelming. You doubt your identity. You are bringing along your "culture" to the group, but the existing group likes their culture just the way it is. You question why you would want to be friends with anyone in this other group. This is where people feel like frauds and begin to experience imposter syndrome.

GROUP BETRAYAL

If you comply with the group's identity and your place within the group, all is well. If you rebel against the status quo, you are shunned. These are the laws of belonging to any group.

When you speak up to help someone penetrate your own dominant group's force field, you earn respect from the person trying to get into your winner group from the loser group.

For instance, consider a Rebel who is a man on the executive team who is fully supportive of the woman joining the group. He sees her value to making the group stronger, increasing the value of the executive group being a winning group. She is grateful to have a champion on the inside paving the way for her.

But that man may also feel the pressure and maybe even anger from the men who don't want that woman to be included. The man has betrayed the unwritten rules of the group, which is to remain homogeneous. He behaves differently than what is expected. The man now runs the risk of being marginalized because of his "betrayal."

SAME GROUP BUT DIFFERENT MEASUREMENTS OF WINNERS AND LOSERS

During the first year of the Trump presidency, rapper Eminem performed a cypher (a freestyle battle) on the BET Hip Hop Awards called "You Ain't My President!" It was a political statement about Eminem's perception of power abuse.

Eminem not only had much to say about the president, but he also called out what he saw as behavior he wouldn't tolerate by his fan base.

And any fan of mine
Who's a supporter of his
I'm drawing in the sand a line
You're either for or against
And if you can't decide
Who you like more and you're split
On who you should stand beside,
I'll do it for you with this [middle finger].
F*CK YOU.

There was a backlash by Eminem fans on Twitter for his cypher.

- Welp! [sic] I'm done with Eminem too. Keep it going celebs. Keep disrespecting Trump supporters, then wonder what happen to your fans and ratings.
- No more respect for Eminem. You can't call out your fans like that. #disappointed
- I was a fan of Eminem. He drew a line in the sand. I'm out. #MAGA (Kelley, 2017)

Eminem's rap delivered a powerful message about his stand on racism, power abuse, and corruption that he saw in America supported by politics. But there are fans of Eminem and fans of Trump. Those who were fans of both had a choice to make. Who they would choose was a result of which group, Trump's or Eminem's, was seen as the winning group versus the losing group based on their point of view.

Renowned rapper, Redman, in an interview, commented on the cypher in a way that is relevant to Smugglers. He articulated how important it was that Eminem represented the sentiment of the "loser" group versus Trump's "winner" group. In Smuggler speak, he points out that it wasn't a "loser" yelling. It was a "winner" agreeing that the "loser" ideals are important.

> *"As I watched that BET cypher, I was like, 'Wow.' You know, Eminem could've went up there and blacked out on rhymes with flows and kilt shit. But, he felt as a person of his color, to represent us on BET with a rhyme addressing the president. Y'all gotta understand that, alright?*
>
> *He's not black. He's white. We all know that. But, he*

has power. And he used this power on that BET cypher to make a statement. For us as well, for all of us as a people.

But especially for us. And everyone, anyone should respect that man for that. Because he didn't have to do it. It's not even many of us that wouldn't even step out the box and did what he did and took that opportunity to use that platform on a BET cypher, and use that platform, to make a mother fucking statement.

And for him to come out on the show to do that. To remember the rhyme. To feel it's a just do as not just Eminem the rapper, but as Marshall Mathers, the person. To step up of my color. To represent the wrong injustice that's going on in America.

And I fucking commend him on that. Not because he is one of my favorites but just the step he took. He could have used that platform to black the fuck out. Like if BET had asked me again that I would have been up there blackin' it the fuck out, I wouldn't have said shit about what is goin' on. I would have been blackin' it.

But he used it to make a statement. And that's one thing we should respect about with that man. He stood up for injustice. For a man of his color. And use that platform to get the point across." (Redman Reacts to Eminem's Freestyle: "He Used His Platform as A White Artist to Stand Up For US!", 2017)

Eminem translated the frustration of social injustice in words that bridged the racial divide, using rap as a channel of communication. He acknowledged how some black people felt and amplified their voice with his platform.

Eminem has a global audience. Losing a part of his fan base that he doesn't want to affiliate with anyway was fine by him.

He has positional power, after all. But, notice that because he didn't do what part of his group expected him to do, he was marginalized by them.

You are a minion who is not in a position of power. If you worked for one of the angry fans tweeting, what might be the repercussions if they knew you supported Eminem? If you don't conform to the group, you could be marginalized at work and lose your job. Or even your career.

Yes. Your career.

LOSING YOUR CAREER

Peter Norman, a white Australian, won a silver medal at the 1968 Mexico City Olympics. He shared the victory dais with gold medal winner, Tommie Smith, and bronze medal winner, John Carlos, two black Americans.

The American Anthem began playing in the stadium per the gold medal win. Fans were singing along, until suddenly, the crowd fell deathly silent. As the song played, the audience saw something shocking. They may not have understood the symbolism of what was going on, but they knew that what they were witnessing on the dais did not conform to what was "normal."*

The American athletes were barefoot to protest poverty. They wore scarves to protest lynching. They wore the athlete's Olympic Project for Human Rights badge in support of the battle for equality around the globe. They lowered their heads in

---

* Diamond, B. (2015, October 10). The White Man in That Photo. Retrieved from Films For Action: http://www.filmsforaction.org/articles/the-white-man-in-that-photo/?utm_medium=google

defiance during the National Anthem and raised their fists in a Black Power salute that rocked the world.

People instinctively follow those who look like they know what they are doing. People bet that they will be a winner if they go along with the confident person leading the group. The crowd not only stopped singing—they started screaming insults, led by the dominant group of whites.

But the story that doesn't get told as often has to do with Peter Norman, the white Australian. Before going up to the podium, he learned about what his fellow medal winners planned to do. He said, *"I believe in what you believe. Do you have another one of those [Olympic Project for Human Rights badges] for me? That way I can show my support in your cause."*

There is a *Life Magazine* photo of the three medalists in the moment. The image is potent. But the fallout of their actions protesting the behavior of the dominant group, was ironic. They were protesting being "less than." Then they were treated more severely than "less than."

The American medalists were ousted from the Olympic Village and suspended from the US team. They were fired from their jobs. They received death threats for their silent protest.

The Australian medalist, on the other hand, was never allowed to compete again in the Olympics, despite qualifying repeatedly. He was shunned and struggled to find work. He could have easily folded, saying, *"I didn't know what was going on around me,"* and been assigned to a cushy committee post with future Olympics. But he didn't. He stood outside of his white group in support of his peers who faced injustice.

Tommie Smith explained his heroism. *"It wasn't just a simple gesture to help us, it was HIS fight. He was a white man, a white Australian man among two men of color, standing up in the moment* *of victory, all in the name of the same thing."** Carlos said, "Not every young white individual would have the gumption, the nerve, the backbone, to stand there."***

In 2012, the Australian government apologized posthumously to Peter Norman in a formal motion, acknowledging the power abuse he suffered and acknowledging his contribution to furthering racial equality.

Bottom line, he stood outside of his "winning" group culture, siding with the "loser" group culture.

COURAGE AND CONSEQUENCES

You see, our American competitive mindset, with winners and losers, is an equilibrium. Groups will repel each other based on their differences. But inside a group, there is cohesion. If a group member stretches too far away from the center, he loses his cohesion to the group and is then on the outs. You will see this play out in politics, in the news, and at your company.

When you try to speak up against your own group to change it from what is to a new way of being, your own peers, boss, or company will try to force you to cohere.

There are group pressures when you don't conform to the status quo. It takes courage for you to step outside of the group and proceed with the "new." It also takes an incredible conviction that what you're doing is the right thing.

---

* Diamond, B. (2015, October 10). The White Man in That Photo. Retrieved from Films For Action: http://www.filmsforaction.org/articles/the-white-man-in-that-photo/?utm_medium=google

** Flanagan, M. (2006, October 10). 'Tell your kids about Peter Norman'. Retrieved from The Age: http://www.theage.com.au/news/national/tell-your-kids-about-peter-norman/2006/10/09/1160246071527.html

THE UNWRITTEN RULES ARE THE RULES

The written code of conduct and the unwritten rules of groups inside of a dysfunctional company are at odds. The unwritten rules of the group dictate the acceptance of behaviors that are not written down but are universally understood. These unwritten rules are then shared by word of mouth, peer to peer. The compelling message with unwritten rules is, do these things in a dysfunctional company and you will get ahead.

If you speak up and push your good idea, you have failed to follow the rule that the Corporate Conformist is the one calling the shots. You are a minion and disobeyed the unwritten rule of don't challenge the status quo. They and their cronies run the show, and you need to knock it off and get back to their priorities, whether your idea can help or not.

Employees are told to speak their minds, take a stand, and take risks. That takes courage. But dysfunctional groups have beaten the courage out of people after they speak up and get smacked into submission. If you complain about the unwritten rules, you aren't showing courage—rather, you appear as a whining complainer who causes problems. Once again, you are friction.

The unwritten rules of the dominant groups mask the genuine issues behind the dysfunction. Do you watch people bully others? Then it is okay to bully others. Do you watch people lie at work? Then it is okay to lie. Do you watch the boss hire their friends? Then it is okay for the boss to hire their friends.

Employee handbooks state that "we embrace diversity," or we have a "policy against retaliation." But these policies have no teeth given the behaviors of employees who discriminate and retaliate. The unwritten rules of the dominant groups impact productivity at work. No one trusts that the written rules will be enforced because there are too many examples that they aren't.

If you find yourself surrounded by these unwritten rule landmines, pay attention and identify where these unwritten rules lie. These are the rules in a dysfunctional company. They are fixed. They should be listed in a handbook that's given to you on day one.

In a work environment, you now know why there are people and groups who consider themselves to be "winners" over the "losers." You now understand the nature of the competitive mindset.

This doesn't make wrong behaviors right or tolerable in any way. As a Rebel, I fully expect you to stand up for what is right.

Rather than speak up against a group, which will likely put you on the outs, it is smarter to *infiltrate that group* and make changes from the inside out. At least if you need to keep your job! After all, you need to stay where you are to affect any sort of change, especially around the unwritten group rules.

Don't worry. I will explain how to avoid these unwritten rules and how to navigate the behavior of Corporate Conformists. I am putting color to these invisible forces that have been working against you, so you have the opportunity to observe them real time at work.

Most people are not ready to be unplugged from the mindset of the rulers and the ruled; the winners and the losers. Many people are so hopelessly dependent on the notion of being better than others that they will fight to protect the existing system. If they aren't a winner against the big dog, at least they can be a winner over you. They fail to see how cooperation lifts all. They fight tooth and nail to maintain the status quo.

What you are going to learn is how to play your cooperative game within their competitive game. Each "loser" like you who joins the "winners" creates the path for others, which effectively alters the power balance. You will infiltrate the dominant group, and the members of that group won't even know that they have embraced the change.

CHAPTER 8

It's Not a Wall. It's a Force Field.

IMAGINE A FORCE FIELD AS A PROTECTIVE SPHERE OF ENERGY encapsulating your body. Now, imagine another person with their protective sphere of energy surrounding them.

When two people who don't know each other stand side-by-side, these force fields meet, and the hum of electricity fills the air. It is like two light sabers touching. In reality, you might just be standing in front of a person. But if you look through the lens of a Smuggler, you will begin to see that all people have a force field protecting their identity.

Force fields are an invisible form of energy that work against people and groups coming together. Force fields matter. They are the unseen barriers you need to lower or penetrate quietly to create the trust and understanding necessary to drive any result.

You see, it isn't the nature of an individual and their identity which creates friction. It is the friction caused by two force fields rubbing against each other. It is the charged energies between people that clash.

When you are upset with someone, it is because what you expect should happen isn't happening. It's not what you would have anticipated inside of your own force field, based on the way that you see the world.

The person in the other force field might suggest that you should do things their way, not your way. The hidden message is that their way is the winning way, and your way is the losing way. Your force field goes up to protect your idea of yourself as a winner. When you push back on the idea, it goes through the same process with the other person, and their force field is raised and then strengthened protecting their identity as a winner.

If you are working with a collaborative team, it is because you have lowered your team members' force fields. You have penetrated the protective shell that surrounds a person's identity. No one on the team thinks that you will attack who they are at their core. They have learned to trust you. They are willing to compromise because they know that you have considered their interests along with your own.

THE VALUE OF UNDERSTANDING IDENTITY AS A FORCE FIELD

Understanding that people will go to great lengths to protect their identity gives Smugglers a *cooperative edge*.

This knowledge provides the opportunity to show how an initiative can enhance a person's identity. Knowing how a person views themselves allows you to support that perspective or, at times, to negate that perspective.

At work, everyone is dressed professionally. Outside of gender and race and ability, everyone appears to belong to the same group. You see one cohesive company team. But those invisible force fields are there. There are departmental groups at odds. There are people who believe that their group is superior—for instance, people who treat cafeteria workers like servants. There are racial force fields. There are gender force fields. All these force fields are in place to protect a person's individual identity and group identity of being a winner, and not a loser.

There is always a potential for force fields to repel others, derailing productive work. People might cooperate with one person but repel another person because their force fields clash. All people have their own self-identity force fields and their corresponding group force fields.

The individual and group force fields that you have around you are the same individual and group force fields that another person has. Smugglers treat each person's identity tenderly and with the utmost respect. You must understand your perspective and expectations, as well as the other person's perspective and expectations, before you can have an opportunity to cooperate.

No one thinks that they are a jerk. They may feel "tough," or "strategic," or "sarcastic," which is why they behave in specific ways. Because we Smugglers understand that a person's identity is the most important thing to them, we know that reflecting that exact identity is the key to bringing people closer to center. Closer to collaboration. Closer to a more representative view of the world. Closer to the cooperative mindset.

It isn't a wall that you are banging your head against repeatedly. It is the electrical force field that Smugglers alone can see.

The good news is that there are always ways to lower or even penetrate force fields.

SOMETIMES A HEAD-ON APPROACH WON'T WORK

Consider Carrie's story. Carrie found a great idea that she knew would benefit her company as well as her department. But, her boss's identity was that he was in charge, and no one could have any ideas which he considered to be "beneath him."

> *"A vendor approached me with a great product that I thought would be a fit for what we were doing in my department. But, I knew he [her VP] would never consider it unless it was his idea. And he would reject it forever if he knew I was the person proposing it.*
>
> *I told the vendor the truth straight out, and said they would have to trust me if they wanted a chance to get in front of him. I told them that they couldn't mention my name if I could get them the meeting. I would be a negative strike against them because he saw me as a threat. They would be on their own if I was successful in getting them into the meeting.*
>
> *So, since I couldn't ask him [the VP], I asked a different VP for help. My VP had a man crush on this guy because he thought he had more clout. He did meet with the higher-ups a lot more.*
>
> *But, Matt [the other VP] was cool. I asked him for a favor when we were in line at Starbucks waiting for coffee. I asked him if he would email him [my VP] the vendor's*

information along with a suggestion that he should talk to them. Matt knew exactly why I was asking.

My VP made the appointment the following week.

The vendor became an approved vendor within the next two months. My VP had no idea that I was the one behind the scenes. He assigned the vendor to me to implement the solution if you can believe that!"

Carrie knew the VP's identity of being a professional-god-allowed-to-engage-only-with-other-gods needed to be satisfied before any progress could be made with the vendor. She managed his expectations of being the smartest guy in the room. She smuggled the solution without him even knowing.

THE SECRET ABOUT WINNING AND LOSING IN AMERICAN CULTURE

We are told we too can be "winners" and beat the odds if we work hard enough. Go out. Get an education. The world is our oyster. Our Constitution states that all men are created equal and have the equal opportunity to succeed in life through hard work. That through our toils and labors, we each have a chance to climb the ladder of success if we try hard enough.

What these people don't tell us is that there is a qualifier. Go and be successful, providing you don't have a job or anything that is "better than mine."

Because if you do well, I look like a loser. They can't let that happen, so they have to block you to maintain their winner status.

WHAT SOME PEOPLE THINK IF YOU TRY TO ENTER THEIR GROUP

Politics pits one group against another. Terrorism pits one group against another. Sunday football pits one group against another. There is no middle. One side believes it is "better" than the other.

What happens when a person from the loser group (a nondominant group), reveals himself to be more talented than a member of the winner group (the dominant group)? If a person believes they are in the winning group, and you are in the losing group, then to "mix" the groups suggests that all members of the combined groups are equal. If that happens, in members of the winning group's minds, they have plummeted down to your loser status.

You have penetrated the force field of the dominant group, as well as the force field protecting the individual member's identity, without invitation. You have amplified the risk of the person from the dominant group losing rank.

A group member cannot allow that to happen. It is at odds with how they view themselves—as being a winner. This person's internal alarm blares, telling them to use their entire arsenal to keep the loser group member out. They will do everything possible to shore up the breach to both make you uncomfortable using words you don't understand and shunning you in their behaviors, so that you eventually leave. They want you to feel so awful you spread the word to others from your loser group that they aren't welcome either.*

These invisible force fields represent the glass ceiling, the

---

* Buss, D., Gomes, M., & Lauterbach, K. (1987, June). Tactics of manipulation. Journal of Personality and Social Psychology. Retrieved from The National Center for Biotechnology Information: https://www.ncbi.nlm.nih.gov/pubmed/3598864

barrier between the poor and rich, the boundary between races, and other divisions. Some people and groups believe that they are better than you. What you must acknowledge is that the ceiling of your group is perceived as the floor of theirs.

When we talk about ceilings and floors, we are automatically creating a mental construct of another group "above" us. If you strip away the values we have applied to winners and losers, you see that it comes down to force fields between people and groups. Ceilings and floors feel solid. But a force field? Well, that can be lowered or penetrated.

Some people have the unfortunate reality of having to lower many more force fields than others. For instance, if you are a woman who is African American, gay, from a poor neighborhood, with a GED, there are:

- Men who think that they are "above" you.
- White people who think that they are above you.
- Straight people who think they are above you.
- Rich people who think they are above you.
- Educated people who think they are above you.

What's worse is that the woman in this situation is taught to think so, too. When you have that many force fields working against you, you just accept that it is how the world works. The odds of smuggling your way out of that situation are daunting.

The situation is similar to a bracket system in sports. If you are in the losing bracket, it means you have to play more rounds than a highly ranked seed to make it to the championship game. If you have ever been in the losing bracket in sports, you know how hard it is to muster the energy for each additional game you have to play.

The losers' bracket is the starting point for Smugglers trying to succeed in a dysfunctional environment. Each game played represents the force fields you have to fight through to get to the next round.

The truth is that you aren't equal in "their" eyes. There are people in dominant groups who are rooting against you, consciously or subconsciously. Invisible forces work against you every single day.

"WINNERS" HAVE AN ADVANTAGE

Many people think they are winners and look down on the losers, when in fact, up to a certain point, many people haven't even "won" on their own merits.

The competition mindset forces the notion of winners and losers between socioeconomic groups, racial groups, gender groups, and other groups. How hard have the winners worked to be the top seed?

The community in which you were born is your starting point in the competition of life. But, winners who won by birthright have a tough time recognizing that they have been given a head start. It's no different than upper management and how they view entry level employees.

When you consider the losers, who have been forced to climb through multiple force fields to get where they are, you start to realize that their efforts take a considerable amount of additional effort. You also realize that they suffer a never-ending battle.

WE DON'T GET KNOCKED DOWN THE LADDER; WE CLIMB DOWN WILLINGLY.

People with the competitive mindset in the dominant group push you back down to your subdominant group, through their floor to your ceiling. Their force field intensifies, and they tell you to try harder. Corporate Conformists say that it is your fault for being deficient and not having the skills that you require to compete within the dominant group and advance your career. They tell you that you are making excuses.

We are complicit in keeping "winners" in power. We believe that we should be "below" them, and they agree. Being ruled is a state of mind that we accept. They push us away, and we eventually give up trying.

WORD FORCE FIELDS

There are members who don't want you in their group. To prevent access, a member will try to shame you into not understanding the nature of how the group functions. They choose their words selectively to emphasize the differences between you and them and to make you feel unwelcome.

Consider the entrepreneurial world at an angel group on a pitch night. What happens at these events is entrepreneurs take twenty minutes to pitch their idea to investors to fund their business. Assume that this particular investor meeting has a high concentration of Corporate Conformists.

You are invited to observe the meeting. You are happy to do so because you want to learn about the entrepreneurial world. A man approaches you after the presentation and asks, "Did you invest in the angel round for the fill-in-the-name-of-your-favorite-startup-here? They are talking about a 10x return based on the proforma." In the event these terms are new to you, it's this elementary: "Did you give that guy money to get his business going? He may or may not pay you back. But, if he does, he'll pay you ten times what you gave him."

If you can speak in his jargon, he'll know that you are part of his investor group. If you're not familiar with the lingo, then you couldn't possibly understand the complexity of his world. He is more knowledgeable about such complicated things because his angel group is superior to your non-angel group. The question is a probe. Are you sophisticated and knowledgeable about me and my fellow members?

Angel investors must be accredited, or able to show an annual income of $200,000 for the last two years. The question from this group member was also an inquiry of your wealth. He is wondering if you are wealthier than him or if he outranks you.

The question also tests your knowledge of a business that hasn't hit the mainstream news. He is wondering, "Do you know more than me? Are you providing more value to the group than my inside track?"

If you answer satisfactorily, your interlocutor might pivot to see how else they can outrank you. For instance, they may also inquire about where you went to college as another measuring stick. If you answer the questions that make you eligible for group membership, perhaps they can beat you with how your school ranks against theirs.

Having an awareness of groups and the competition mindset allows us to choose our behavior. We have the opportunity to strategically plan how to lower a member of the winning group's force field by respecting their winning identity.

YOU CAN RAISE FORCE FIELDS TOO

The other side of the coin is a purposeful raising of the force field.

Going back to the Eminem example, he chose to raise the force field of the group he identified with—those who are anti-Trump. By making this distinction of being different than Trump supporters, he also made people choose to be inside or outside of that force field.

His statement meant that you were a winner if you agreed with him and a loser if you didn't. Trump's fans don't want to think of themselves as losers, so the option was to stop being a fan of Eminem.

They were repelled by Eminem's force field.

CURRENT SOLUTIONS AREN'T EFFECTIVE

What happens when you are frustrated with a coworker and the conversation becomes heated? Current HR solutions, such as psychological assessments, are insufficient. Have you stopped to think, okay that person is an introverted intuitive according to Myers Briggs? Do you think, "Hold on. Let me interrupt my racing thoughts during the conflict to see if I can confirm that you scored high on the D, CD, Di, and i scales and low on the S, CS, and C scales of a DiSC profile?"

No.

With all due respect to the value of these tools, they don't help at all when I'm frustrated and ready to cut out of a meeting and walk to the bar to calm myself down.

You are thinking about how to resolve the problem immediately in front of you. No change management program or leadership course will help you in a dysfunctional system because those methods of training focus on an individual's nature. They don't take into consideration how a person views the world through their personal identity and group affiliation.

What they *really don't do* is explain how to manage the heat felt between two people who haven't had that training in ten years.

What is needed is a system to understand the energies between people. A system that isn't so complicated that you need a certification to understand it. Something that is so instinctual that you can pivot the minute you sense tensions or when different players walk into the room.

LOWERING FORCE FIELDS

Smuggling is an interpersonal strategy to lower force fields. A Smuggler minimizes a person's internal resistance to a new idea while simultaneously increasing their own confidence. Then the Smuggler must reduce the friction between themselves and the opposing individual or group so that the idea is brought to life unscathed.

Conflict happens when there isn't reciprocity or respect for the other person's identity. Trust is built only as each force field comes down. By lowering force fields, you get to a place of mutual respect and then cooperation in solving everyday problems.

The way to lower a force field is to reflect the opposing party's identity back onto themselves. You want them to feel confident enough to let down their force field because you have no obvious judgements against who they think they are.

Some people will say this is finding common ground with someone. Not quite. Finding common ground with someone is important. But that is not what I'm referencing. Some people will say that you are just telling someone what they want to hear. But that's not it, either.

In the Harry Potter series, character Draco Malfoy is Harry's enemy. Draco is a bully. He and his family identify as members of the dominant group—pure-blood wizards. These are the bad guys.

In one scene, Harry confronts Draco and his mother, who indoctrinated Draco with her beliefs that pure-bloods are superior. Draco's mother insults Harry, and he responds, *"They might be able to find you a double cell in Azkaban [Wizard Prison] with your loser of a husband!"* Draco gets in between them and yells, *"Don't you dare talk to my mother like that, Potter!"*

We know Draco is a terrible bully. But, with this sentence, he reveals a critical part of his identity—loyalty to his family. His force field tells him that his actions of preparing to fight Harry are perfectly acceptable because his identity of being loyal to his family and his pure-blood group have been threatened.

Now, in the books, Harry was in high school and wasn't exactly trying to advance initiatives with a cooperative approach. So, we will substitute you in this case for what you could do, if you worked on a project with Draco.

People who say to "find common ground" have likely not considered that you'd be hard-pressed to find common ground with a wizard traitor. You don't need to find common ground. What you need is for him to cooperate. Your purpose is to have him help you drive your initiative.

You aren't going to agree with Draco that he is superior, and you aren't going to commend him on his brilliance at being a bully as a way to lower his force field.

To lower his force field, you home in on the value of the behavior he demonstrated as important to him—protecting his mother. You choose to focus on reflecting his identity of being clever, smart, and loyal to his family.

Before you can have Draco contribute positively to your project, you are going to have to take the initiative to try to lower his force field.

You might say, "Draco, there is something I observed the other day when things got a bit heated. But I wanted to let you know that you revealed something that was really commendable. You defended your mother and were ready to throw. That showed your loyalty to your family. Your parents must be very proud."

This is an approach that has the potential to have Draco let down his force field, even though it would only be a smidge (he is a really big bully). He would probably say something like, "What are you getting at?" You can then tell him sincerely that it was just a statement. You have successfully reflected his most prized, and vulnerable, self—that he is a fiercely loyal person to his family. You may have even exceeded his expectations, creating a glimmer of a positive feeling anchored to you.

Because you have sincerely acknowledged this admirable part of his identity, you have lowered your own force field of judgment about his jerkish behavior. You have accessed his force field through a side door. This vulnerability is what builds trust—a critical element of changing someone's mind. Not to mention that you may have also exceeded his expectations about this encounter, making him feel slightly more positive about engaging with you.

You don't try to advance your initiative at this point. You only try to let your antagonist experience the positive feelings of your compliment. You may reapproach him at another time, allowing him to remember his either neutral or exceeded expectations of how you engaged him.

Smugglers allow Corporate Conformists to maintain their

identity of being a "winner" while operating within the Smuggler's cooperative model.

SMUGGLING PREMISE

The dominant group will not willingly join a nondominant group—which is why smuggling is the only choice in a closed and dysfunctional system. Smugglers must lower the force fields to have a chance to penetrate the membership of the group. The opportunity for a cooperative approach begins with this quiet infiltration of a nondominant member into the group.

People will engage outside of the Smuggler's purview. This is why Smugglers make educated guesses about the tensions that exist between other people and the potential impact those tensions might have on the project. Because you understand how each person sees his or her own identity, you anticipate what is needed to lower those walls before you even start. (More on this later in the book.)

CHAPTER 9

A Method to Changing Stubborn Minds

WE ARE BOMBARDED ALL DAY LONG WITH INPUT FROM MAGAZINES, newspapers, TV, conversations, advertisements—you name it. This input, whether it take the form of an article, a blog, or a soundbite, always begins with a headline.

We are a headline culture. If a person consumes a headline, it sticks in their mind as being true. If there is no other input challenging that headline, then it stays in a perpetual state of being true in a person's mind. The headlines support the existing position.

Smugglers work to change the headline when there is new information to the contrary. However, because they aren't a source from TV or the internet, they must invest the time required to gently change the minds of those convinced that they are right.

HOW IDENTITY AND HEADLINES WORK TOGETHER

I just read a headline from the internet. "Trump unscripted and unleashed."

If I am a conservative and I post this on my Facebook page, my conservative friends might comment, "Isn't that awesome! He is really changing the game in DC." If I am a liberal and I post this on my Facebook page, my liberal friends might say, "He is totally unhinged." The headline reflects how a person feels about a situation based on their personal identity.

When people's comments don't jibe with the way "I" perceive the headline, there is friction. They are actually passing judgment on me with their comment. They think I have it wrong. That puts up defensive walls immediately for those who are passionate supporters of a headline.

But a headline can also come from your workplace. Take, for example, two team members who have different ideas about how to advance the goals of a committee. They might interpret a directive of "Create an Innovation Council" with two totally different notions about the function. Both think they are right.

GROUPS SUPPORT HEADLINES

The members of our group tell us what we should value. If a headline in the news appeals to a person, it is because it reflects positively upon their identity in the group. Headlines can be jargon, online content, or even the gossip of the day. When we share information with others in our group, it satisfies our internal needs of belonging and external needs of being recognized for our value.

In the era of social media, our need for status in a group has intensified polarization—I'm right, you're wrong. Our curiosity about the other person's perspective, and desire to bridge whatever divide we perceive, has given way to belonging to a group and measuring our status through likes and shares.

Carl, a geologist, pointed out, *"It can be challenging to come to a resolution with some people. Many people do not know how to take a difference of opinion and find a happy medium."*

Fifty-nine percent of people forward emails based on headlines that support their identity without reading the content.* That is a crazy number. Now, given the speed of a click, a headline that reflects an identity can be shared with anyone instantaneously, whether it is truthful or not.

How do you differentiate who is one of the 59 percent who forward content with a click, from the 41 percent who check to see if things are real?

INTENSITY OF FEELINGS

Reading a headline that I perceive to be correct, or that particularly resonates with me, gives me a spring in my step for the day. It

---

* Demers, J (2016, August 8). 59 Percent Of You Will Share This Article Without Even Reading It. Retrieved from Forbes: https://www.forbes.com/sites/jaysondemers/2016/08/08/59-percent-of-you-will-share-this-article-without-even-reading-it/#198025222a64

also provides me ammo to challenge someone who might harbor a different point of view. The headline "proves" I'm right.

But, when I read a headline that questions my identity, or suggests that I'm wrong or in a "losing" group, I experience the opposite. These types of negative feelings are what ultimately lead to angry social media shares, mean comments, and sometimes public protests or even violent acts. It also results in bullying or passive-aggressive behaviors in the office.

The bottom line is that these negative headlines translate into negative action. The cycle of trying to show that I am the winner and the other team is the loser continues on an endless loop, creating a contagion.

It takes twelve positive experiences to make up for one unresolved negative experience. You will have to try twelve times harder to bring a person around to your way of thinking if they experience a negative affiliation with you (a post, a position, or a decision they may not agree with). If maintaining the relationship with that person is important to you, you will have to offer twelve positive reasons to offset the negative experience.[*]

A NEGATIVE REFLECTION OF A PERSON'S IDENTITY CHANGES BEHAVIORS

It is why political ads trend negatively. When you see any headline that is opposite to the way you view the world and how it "should" be, it feels like a blow to your identity. When the

---

[*] McGovern, M. (2012, June 21). How long does one bad experience last in a customer's mind? Retrieved from Customer Experience Insight: http://www.customerexperienceinsight.com/how-long-does-a-bad-experience-last-in-a-customers-mind/

headline inherently opposes something that is very important to you—for instance, people who are motivated to vote against candidates with different views—you become ticked off enough to take action.

A negative reflection on your identity can also motivate you to change your behavior and switch brands. For instance, the beer you used to drink in college may not be your brand of choice today. The old brand no longer reflects your identity, and the new one, at this point in your life, does.

At work, the headline could be your project. But if the person you are talking to really doesn't care about the results of your project because it doesn't reflect meaningfully upon his or her identity, then you can be assured that the project is DOA.

DUNNING-KRUGER EFFECT

There is a cognitive bias called the Dunning-Kruger effect. This bias considers the force field tensions between people who overestimate their smarts with people who underestimate their smarts. In today's polarized world, this creates winners and losers before the game even starts.

The theory centers on the differences between competence and incompetence.

Competent people have evolving opinions about their points of view because there is always new input from varied sources. People who believe there is more to know, and question the facts, presume that other people have evolving opinions too based on new input.

Incompetent people form the wrong conclusions based on outdated information, or more importantly, the way they feel about past experiences regarding the subject matter. They overestimate their intellect and can't recognize the faults in their thinking. They don't even suspect that there could be any more information to change their point of view. They fail to factor in how things have evolved, how things will evolve in the future, or that they may even have their information wrong. They believe they know all about the issue based on their subjective experiences and end up making bad decisions.

So they motor along, thinking that they are the smartest person in the room and far superior to anyone else. Their confidence in their point of view trumps their actual knowledge. These are the people who keep inertia going strong.

An example of competence would be a CEO who listens to customer feedback in addition to how his executive team envisions the future. He takes in many perspectives before forming a conclusion. Jeff Bezos, CEO of Amazon, who serves over 164 million customers, built a company from the ground up based off the core philosophy of helping the customer at all cost, making decisions based on customer feedback. This ongoing input from customers would be an example of competence.

Apple introduced the personal computer in 1977. Ken Olsen, the founder of Digital Equipment Corporation, said soon after, "There is no reason anyone would want a computer in their home." (Ironically, DEC was eventually acquired by Compaq—a personal computer company.) People who fail to take in new information to evaluate how it fits into the future context of a situation meet the criterion of incompetence.

But the terms competent and incompetent can only take our argument so far. People are competent in some facets of their life and incompetent in others. We all harbor errant points of view because we are not as logical as we think we are. Humans are naturally irrational, and we make decisions based on how we feel.

As such, I have chosen to use a new construct. I now think of someone who is incompetent as a "headlines only" reader, or put simply, a *headliner*.

On the other hand, I think of a person who is competent as one who seeks out various sources to challenge his or her perspective. I view these types of people as *researchers*.

Understanding if a person is a headliner or a researcher will tell you how much time you need to put in to unwind their current perspective and change their minds. This time is necessary if your ultimate goal is to cause someone to question how their current perspective might put their identity in jeopardy. Once they are in a state of uncertainty, you can offer your position, or project solution, as the way for them to rebalance and confirm their self-identity.

HEADLINERS

Headliners represent anyone who goes along blindly with what other members of their group are saying. When you present a headline that opposes a headliner's identity, they can dig in their heels and say, "Your facts are wrong," regardless of your reputable sources.

Headliners lead with emotion and support their views subjectively with facts that fit their argument. If a fact doesn't jibe with their point of view, they dismiss it. Logic fails to persuade a headliner.

A HEADLINER'S STARTING POINT —CIRCULAR REASONING

Circular reasoning is where the conclusion of an argument is included in the premise—for instance, in the phrase, "healthcare is expensive." The foregone conclusion that healthcare is expensive is a person's starting point. In any circular argument, the false starting point prevents productive conversations.

Headliners don't know that they are using circular reasoning by sharing headlines. They are just perpetuating the position for others in the group who don't question the validity of the headline either.

People who question healthcare's price and profit margins versus costs in a competitive market are met with skepticism. The people who challenge the reasoning *must not understand that healthcare is expensive.* After all, everyone knows that healthcare is expensive, and if you think that way, you are part of a winning group of people who understand the industry better than you, a loser for thinking differently.

If you prove that your information is correct, the person you're interacting with may backpedal to defend his or her perspective. "That isn't what I/s/he/it meant," they'll allege, intimating that you don't understand the intention of the information they shared.

Headliners also say things like:

- *The market isn't going to change.*
- *We looked at that vendor six years ago and ruled them out.*
- *It's better to keep the process we have. Everyone understands how things work right now.*

They no longer question the knowledge. If they do search for more insights, they skim the headlines. They only pay attention to information that supports their existing opinion. They then use this information to make decisions.

If you run into a headliner who thinks this way, you know what to expect. Their point of view is fixed. It is their "truth." They absorbed information and gave feelings to their convictions. Once they feel confident, their point of view is more-or-less frozen in place.

RESEARCHERS

There is an old adage that says, "You are defined by the people who surround you." I would like to extend that notion to include the fact that you are represented by the knowledge you put into your own head and the words that spill from your mouth.

It occurred to me that despite all the knowledge in the world, a person still only learns things one bite at a time. Knowledge exists in the world. But it isn't in a person's head until they are taught or teach themselves.

A person who "critically-reads-the-whole-article-providing-a-different-perspective-to-shape-their-opinion" is what I call a "researcher." This heuristic differentiates the people who will critically think about information. They form their own opinions versus claiming someone else's headline as theirs. This independent research is what supports their identity.

Researchers focus on learning more about a subject to ensure their point of view is accurate and up to date. These people realize that time and context changes everything. They end up reaching correct conclusions but still question whether they are right or wrong. They lack the confidence to say, "This is how it is." They think there could be more information that they might be missing—even if they are the expert. As a result, these folks can explain problems, as well as solutions, in depth.

Researchers say things like:

- *Is this technology still working for us?*
- *Is our current customer still the right customer for our growth?*
- *Will our product be of value three years from now?*
- *We looked at that vendor six years ago, let's see how their thinking has changed.*

This way of thinking is also what makes researchers more valuable in times of crisis. They are better equipped to manage uncertainty because they have studied all the routes to solutions. Their knowledge base is vast. They can rule out less likely scenarios around the problems because they have more variables to consider.

Infallibility is the difference between a headliner and a researcher.

Revive your curiosity. Become a researcher. Share multiple perspectives on a subject so people can see all sides of a story. Investigate research rather than quote the headlines of the day. Prioritize your time to read and learn. Then teach that knowledge to others. Invite pushback on your ideas. It will improve your critical thinking. It will also build your confidence.

FOUNDATIONAL EROSION

Changing a headliner's point of view is an art of seduction. You don't run in to their office and boldly proclaim that things are going to change; you must first adopt more of an interpersonal strategy.

When trying to convince a headliner, logic and facts don't matter. If you challenge a person's ingrained assumptions, they think you are dumb.

To change a headliner's mind, you need to talk to them as a headliner but stay authentic to your researcher self. You must position other headlines as a question, allowing the headliner with whom you're speaking to defend why his position is valid. The objective of your conversations isn't to win. It is to lead.

To change a stubborn mind, you are going to have to remove power from the equation. You should not seek to prove them wrong. You aren't looking for a gotcha moment. You want to avoid an "I know best" conversation. Negative feelings that you create around their self-identity ruins any chances for change.

Your objective is to plant a seed of doubt about the validity of their arguments. You want to poke holes in their assumptions. Not about how they arrived at a conclusion, but why the conclusion is still valid. You plant a seed that resistant minds will water on their own. You are creating self-doubt, one tiny step at a time.

Ask them questions and allow them to reach the conclusion on their own. People learn and build confidence when they fight to understand something. Not too hard that they quit, but enough that they reach for the answer. People become emotionally invested when they figure things out for themselves. Solving problems, after all, is what builds confidence in what they know for sure. They become the source of their headline, especially with other headliners.

You challenge through asking open-ended questions about why the person's original position is still solid. If this piece of information is flawed, do they want it to be attached to their core identity? That is what you are aiming to achieve—doubt in their original position.

LOWER YOUR FORCE FIELD —AGREE WITH THEM

We can allow ourselves to be who we are without putting down others and feeling like we are superior. A person may not have the same point of view as you, but you can seek to understand how their beliefs reflect their identity. We must lower anyone's force field first before we try to change their outlook. More important, we need to respect the person's identity. It is the only path to cooperation.

To change a headliner's point of view from theirs to yours, the first thing you must do is point out how they're right. When you listen and agree with their point of view, they are less likely to perceive you as a threat to their identity. Ask sincere questions to understand the basis of their argument. There is always an underlying logic, and it can usually be acknowledged positively.

For instance, let's consider a situation where you are reintroducing a vendor solution for your company problem. Your boss is a headliner who scoffs when you mention the name of the vendor company. He might say he didn't like the CEO, or that the product wasn't aligned with what the company needed, or that considering them is a waste of time. Your goal is to lower resistance, so you agree with him. Consider the following:

- I didn't like the CEO
  You are right. The former CEO had a horrible reputation. It was smart to not do business with them when he was in charge.
- Their services weren't aligned with our strategic mission
  You are right. We were both on different tracks back

then. You were smart to pass on that opportunity, so we could focus on our priorities at the time.

- Don't waste your time on them. Or my time for that matter
You are right. There was so much wheel spinning the last time we were engaged with them.

When you agree with a person's perceived image of themselves, you create a sense of cooperation and respect. They understand that you respect them for thinking the way that they do. They believe that they are rational and that you would have made the same decision if you were them. That makes you appear logical, too. When people sense that you aren't a threat, they learn to let down their guard.

Your acknowledgment validates their opinion of themselves. They are reflecting their identity as being smart, funny, strong, and able to add value to the conversation. Your positive response in acknowledging their identity allows them to lower their force fields to consider your perspective, as well. It creates the opportunity for a dialogue where they have social permission to change their point of view if they learn new things. You are both in agreement and are seeing eye to eye. No one party has power over the other when you are both in this state.

You are not enemies; you are equals.

CHANGE A HEADLINER WITH THEIR OWN INFORMATION

Approach lowering a headliner's force field from a perspective that is not obvious. Say, for example, that you are talking with someone who is an NRA member and who tells you that it isn't guns who kill people; it is people who kill people.

If you are against guns, you will not have any kind of constructive dialogue with this person if you try to lecture him on why he should think the same way. If you fight headline to headline, you will lose.

But you *can* speak to him about a genuine concern, such as the demographics of suicide-related gun violence.

First you agree, then you present the neutral information.

> *"I agree. You are right. It is people who kill people.*
> *Hey, I just read a statistic that shocked me. Fifty-one percent of total gun deaths in the US are caused by suicide. I also learned that white men accounted for 70 percent of suicides. Is the NRA doing anything to help minimize the suicides of NRA members or create awareness?"*

This person may or may not have known this fact. But what has happened is that you have created incongruity with the person's group identity. They ask themselves, "If I didn't know this, is my position still valid?"

You have repositioned the conversation from who is right versus who is wrong to one where potential solutions can be explored. The statistic isn't about winning. You use headlines as a starting point to bridge understanding. You use this starting point to open his mind to even engage in a dialogue about guns that is mutually respectful, without putting down the other person's stance. Because of this dialogue, you now know even more about this person's self-identity. You may also learn something that you didn't know before, changing your own opinion. Understand that we too are biased based on how we think the world "should" work.

Yes, this is a simplistic example. The point is that you must make someone uncomfortable enough for them to willingly change their beliefs and subsequent behaviors. You want them to explore the aspects on their own. You want to make them curious about your facts so they then become a researcher and not a headliner.

Now, there are NRA members who will flat out say that the stated fact isn't true. That suicides don't happen that much or some other subjective feeling. For many people, the facts you have presented has created too much uncertainty to deal with, and that person will fight to protect their identity as being right no matter what. Flat denials. Calling you names. Fist fights. You have struck, not a nerve, but THE nerve.

That is understandable. Understand that some people are so firmly entrenched in their beliefs about how the world works that they are not ready to be unplugged from their mindset.

To become unplugged implies the need for that person to punch themselves squarely into the heart of how they define themselves. They are forced to face the negative aspects of what they believed and how it was a part of their identity as a whole.

Your strategy to lower the force field is your initial work. It is like blowing one hole in the base of their fortress. Remember, if you did it once, you can do it again. You have created the opportunity for a new foundation, upon which you can build all your other arguments.

Just make sure that you listen because you want whomever you speak with to dent your foundation, as well. It is only from a place of cooperation that people are able to create a mutual understanding, a solid foundation between one another.

NEUTRAL WAYS TO CREATE CRISIS IN A HEADLINE

You can use headlines to sway a person to exhibit different behavior. For example, when you recognize a person's rationale as above average, they experience positive feelings. *"Nice job Jimmy. That really took some clever thinking on your part. Well done. No one else could have done that in the company."* Jimmy is inclined to continue the same behavior and way of thinking.

On the other hand, to create internal crisis you can openly regard a person's conclusion as totally average, or sub-par. One way to do this is to link his or her conclusion to someone they do not hold in high regard, like a fictitious VP named Karen who has a weak reputation. You can say, *"I was talking to Karen. She shares your opinion, Jimmy."* When you link a person's identity to someone he or she dislikes, you also make him them want to distance themselves from that person's perspective, toward your way of thinking.

The compliment to a person's identity is the carrot which rewards their thinking. The stick thwacks their thoughtless acceptance of other people's headlines, especially those who they don't hold in high regard. But once that seed is planted, it creates doubt about how that behavior reflects upon their identity. It is hard for them to repair that crack in their mind.

HOW IDENTITY IS USED TO CHANGE BEHAVIOR AT WORK

How can you use negative reflection to alter the negative behavior of a person or people in a group? How can you use the power of meeting or not meeting the expectations around a person's identity to change their behavior at work?

Judy, a Smuggler who worked at a governmental agency, changed behavior by focusing on identity. Judy told me, *"One example involved open cases that had been open for years. This allowed for projects to linger where staff used the list of active cases to demonstrate how hard they were working. I have four hundred cases to work on; I can't take on more.*

Encouraging the staff to get them closed didn't work all that well because there were no repercussions if they weren't closed. So, I created a tracking system that tracked each open case to completion. Each month an email went out showing everyone's open cases. As no one wanted to be the person with the most open cases, the problem corrected itself."

IDENTITY TRIGGERS AREN'T ALWAYS OBVIOUS

Sometimes, what you think is a negative quality IS a Corporate Conformist's identity. You would think, for example, that by calling someone a slick politician, the negative connotation of the words would make them want to change their behavior. But to that person, being called a slick politician is a compliment. They see their "slickness" as winning in political chess.

For that person to demonstrate a different behavior, the trigger that you could use would be to tell them how they are losing the political chess game—how they are not acting like a strategic thinker.

But be very careful, Smuggler—you have the knowledge to use this technique, but be aware that it can backfire if it is seen as an attack on a person's identity versus a prompting. You have to be cognizant of how you are perceived when using these tools.

WHY PATIENCE IS ESSENTIAL

Change, enlightenment, and engagement happen one mind at a time. But a smart Smuggler knows not all people are ready to be blown away by ideas right off the bat.

Getting a headliner to think differently about something is akin to putting yourself on a diet. It might make you irritable. It might frustrate you. It is slow, but if you are consistent, you will progress. Advance the idea by one point each time you engage with the person. There are many layers involved with a person's identity. Be gentle with your approach.

You will either frustrate yourself or fail at changing a headliner's mind if you don't dig deep and find the patience to have these conversations. Effectively changing someone's mind requires a commitment of your energy, determination, and time.

Your patience forces you to listen and to consider their point of view. After all, you may be the one who is wrong. You might need to reflect on what your perspective means to *your* identity, as well.

THE SUBCONSCIOUS WAY THAT WE PUT DOWN OTHERS

Marshall Goldsmith is one of my favorite authors. He is also the world's number one leadership thinker and number one executive coach. He has many global bestsellers, like his books *Triggers* and *What Got You Here Won't Get You There.*

I watched a video by Marshall where he focuses on words that kill conversations. Most people will try to convince others that their position is right using the words "no," "but," or "however." It doesn't matter how nicely someone says these words—if they use them as a sentence starter, what they are essentially saying is, "my way is right, and yours is wrong."

Other sentence starters that achieve the same I'm-smarter-than-you-are tone include "You Should," "You Need To," and "Obviously."

- You should like Trump *(Because your current view is wrong)*
- You need to learn more about Hillary *(Because you have no idea about why she is better, but I do)*
- The United States is the greatest country on earth. Obviously. *(Because you are obtuse and can't see that on your own.)*

These statements create an immediate defensive wall. "You should" means that you are a loser and don't know the best way to do something, so I will tell you, because my perspective is superior and I'm a winner. Obviously.*

To change a headliner's point of view, eliminate these words from your vocabulary today. Actually, don't use these words with anyone. You will stand out from the rest!

---

* Ni, P. (2006). How to Communicate Effectively and Handle Difficult People. Retrieved from Ni Preston: http://www.nipreston.com/publications/excerpts/How_to_Handle_FINAL_2006-SAMPLE.pdf

CHAPTER 10

The Hardwiring Insights You Need to Know

NOT EVERYONE IS CUT OUT TO BE THE "LEADER." IN OUR MERIT-based society, people often don't understand that. We were sent off to college with the notion that everyone can be a winner if they just try hard enough. Winners are leaders and leaders are in management, according to conventional wisdom. We don't ask ourselves if we are happy; we ask if we are winning.

No one told us about the joy we might experience in merely contributing our best to a team. Passion is when you get to do what you love, in a way where you can show off your "stuff." It isn't enough to work at a company unless you are contributing in a way that is enjoyable.

If I were hired at Google to process expense reports, I would die. I would go to work late each day because I would dread facing a pile of receipts. However, if I worked with Astro Teller in the Moonshots department, my goodness, how much fun would that be? I love thinking of novel approaches and researching projects, figuring out how they could work. I would want to contribute to the success of a team like that. I would be energized because my hardwiring is aligned with the work. It would be fun because I know I'm good at it. My expectations of myself would be realized.

Job insecurity increases when a person is not doing what he enjoys. A person is wound tight when he knows that others are naturally better at the work. People take measures to hide that fact because they are fearful that they will look "less than." Less than another person's group, or less than in their own group via their ranking. Take the example of someone who is super friendly and has a high need to be liked by others, who is made responsible for bill collections. The mismatch of being hardwired for harmony versus playing a tough guy creates tension in that person's mind and in engaging with people at work.

People enjoy contributing to a team in many ways. A group becomes a team when they work together to the best of their abilities to achieve a common goal. When people follow through on what they say they are going to do, they build trust amongst their group. The root of harmony is when people show genuine respect for the unique gifts that others bring to the table. Conversely, if a person is not respected for how she contributes to the team, then friction develops.

When you learn about your hardwiring, you will see why you are either happy or not so happy in your current role. You might enjoy your industry but not understand why you don't like your job. Now stop and think about the other members of your team. Couldn't this be true for them, too?

Bad teaming is the worst. In some situations, certain people take over and do the work and don't want your input. In other instances, no one does anything. Sometimes the people disappear or fail to contribute. You see, few people get to choose their teams. Most of the time you are selected for one by factors out of your control. Sometimes your team rocks, sometimes your team stinks, and sometimes your team limps along. When bad teaming happens, you want nothing more than for that experience to be over.

Titles and job descriptions aren't as crucial as hardwiring when advancing change. There are many people in positions where the job description doesn't align with their natural hardwiring, creating a subconscious sense of uncertainty.

There is no such thing as a bad hardwiring. But there are bad job fits because of hardwiring.

WHAT IS A PERSON'S HARDWIRING?

Understanding hardwiring requires inductive reasoning. Observing people's behavior allows you to predict what they will do in the future. Further, smuggling utilizes heuristics—mental shortcuts. Smugglers need to assess situations quickly to advance ideas on the fly. It is mission critical to read the dynamics between people, which can change instantly depending on who walks into the room.

In teaming, personalities are irrelevant. What is more important is how they want to contribute in a way that aligns with their natural way of being.

Demonstrating respect for the value a person brings to the table builds trust. If you have taken the time to understand how a person wants to contribute to the effort based on their role, and you let them do that, you will move mountains. Understanding a person's expectations of themselves (do they expect that they can or can't) allows you to demonstrate respect for their natural hardwiring. Olivia, an auditor, said, *"Take advantage of each person's gifts, and give credit when it is due. You can accomplish much, and people don't feel threatened by other's performance."*

All people want to contribute to a team in a way that is fun and showcases their strengths. People are hardwired with these abilities when they are born. There are four unique hardwiring traits: big-picture vision, knowledge about how to do things, taking action and getting it done, and building a community within the team. These traits advance business ideas from concept to completion.

This all sounds fine on an intellectual level, but what does it mean in practical terms? To understand, let's look at these four unique hardwiring traits a bit closer.

VISIONARY

"The future of humanity is going to bifurcate in two directions: Either it's going to become multi-planetary, or it's going to remain confined to one planet and eventually there's going to be an extinction event,"[*] said Elon Musk, CEO of SpaceX, CEO of Tesla Motors, and founder of Solar City and PayPal.

If someone thinks like this, you can pretty much guarantee that they are a Visionary. You don't even need to pay attention

[*] Tweney, D. (2013, May 29). What's next from Elon Musk? Warp drives, and colonizing Mars. Retrieved from Venture Beat: https://venturebeat.com/2013/05/29/elon-musk-dreams-big/

to the types of questions that they ask to winnow the choice. However, if you happen to be in a meeting with someone that you don't know, you can tell if they're a Visionary by the questions they ask. The questions that Visionaries ask sound like:

- *What if we could...?*
- *What is the impact long term?*
- *What are the global implications of...?*

Visionaries dream about the future and new ways to change the world. They are big-picture story sellers who attract others to their vision. These people feel respected and appreciated when others want to talk about the big picture and speak in future terms.

Are you a Visionary?

- Do you obsess about a particular business opportunity or industry?
- Do you think of how the future of your industry will look five years down the road?
- Do you think about who you need to network with to bring your vision to life? Not just now, but in the future?
- Do you find people that are not involved in your business or industry less interesting unless they bring value to your vision?
- Do you contribute to conversations to shape the overall idea to make it even better?

When a Smuggler in a company is moving an idea, he must speak in the Visionary's language. For instance, when you want to influence a Visionary, you don't talk about today's task list.

That is tactical lingo. You want to speak in strategic language—how your project will benefit the organization in the future. Talk about how the project will fit into her vision. Allow her to apply her mind to contribute to the idea. You can't have the entire solution worked out, or she won't be able to add her "genius."

KNOWERS

"I found in one of the tombs an inscription saying, 'If you touch my tomb, you will be eaten by a crocodile and hippopotamus.' It doesn't mean the hippo will eat you; it means the person really wanted his tomb to be protected," joked Zahi Hawass, Egyptian archaeologist, Egyptologist, and former Minister of State for Antiquities Affairs.*

He knows all the stories about the people who reigned. The people who served the pharaohs, the commoners. Those cat mummies. The pottery. Dr. Hawass is not only a scientist but also a businessman who has attracted tourism to Egyptian museums. To top it off, he is famous for his wide-brimmed hat and style of dress, similar to that of Indiana Jones.

This type of person is knowledge-oriented. He knows where to find the missing puzzle pieces, and how to connect the dots that no one else has considered. Knowers are aware of efforts that have worked or not worked in the past, as well as from other industries. Because they have "connection minds," they can make the most of the resources at hand and figure out ways to apply them.

Knowers use statements like:

* Radford, T. (2003, November). The King of the Pharaohs. Retrieved from The Guardian: www.theguardian.com/education/2003/nov/27/research.highereducation

- *I know someone who...*
- *It could work if...*
- *We tried this about ten years ago.*

Know that these people have extensive networks and have seen a lot more than the average person.

Are you a Knower?

- Are you more curious than the average person?
- Do people come to you when they don't know where to find information? Is it fun for you to find it?
- Do you have a natural knack for knowing how to connect the dots and how to make things work?
- Does it drive you nuts when you can't figure something out?
- Do you remember things for much longer than the average person?

Knowers love to learn. They are the ones who go to conferences and attend sessions because they hope to learn something new. Or they make connections in markets that are new to them. These are the explorers who go out and find things, who can cobble together solutions because they have seen so much from other industries. They are the finders and curators of knowledge.

If you are working with a Knower, you want to engage him with your need for information and resources to make the project successful. Traditional project deliverables or timelines aren't what a Knower wants. What will be of interest to this leader is how he can contribute to his catalog of helpful tips. Tell him what you think you want, and he will bring you back what you need.

DOERS

"And where I excel is ridiculous, sickening, work ethic. You know, while the other guy's sleeping? I'm working," promised Will Smith, an actor, comedian, producer, rapper, and songwriter.*

Will Smith has appeared in over thirty-seven movies to date, despite being born on September 25, 1968. People who are Doers get a lot done.

Doers are phenomenal at tactics and execution. Not only do they formulate action plans and to-do lists, but they get it done. They are fantastic at delegating and follow-up and snapping the whip to make sure the project is done on time. They are well-organized and fix things down to the last detail.

Doers use statements like:

- *I'll make a list*
- *I'll have that done by tomorrow*
- *I can fix this*

Doers get 'er done. Just give them the task and get out of their way. They do not need micromanagement. They have more ideas on how to tend to every detail than the three other hardwirings. Let 'em run with the ball!

Are you a Doer?

- Do you make lists of things that need to get done with precision and dates of completion?
- Do calendars or Gantt charts excite you?

---

* Kroft, S. (2007, November 30). Will Smith My Work Ethic is Sickening. Retrieved from 60 Minutes: https://www.cbsnews.com/news/will-smith-my-work-ethic-is-sickening/

- Are you most satisfied when something is completed?
- Do you like to fix things?
- Can you handle multiple tasks in succession?

Are you the kind of person who says, "Just give me that and get out of my way" but in a way that makes others happy to let you take over?

If you are working with a Doer, he will want to talk through all the details. Have you thought about the dates, the times, the agendas for the day of something that might not roll out for six months? The reason he is asking you about this is because he is naturally oriented to think this way. He does not care about the vision long term or the resources you will need to get there. He focuses on the details of the exact day that you will roll out this program.

When working with a Doer, use crystal clear and efficient language, like words involving action and times. The words start, stop, go/no go will be especially useful to you. Stage gates are very helpful for Doers when tasks are assigned in each stage. This way, she can check off the tasks and precisely record all that has been achieved based on what she values.

TEAMERS

"I have learned so many great lessons working with many great leaders. It's hard to say what the best [lesson] is, but one of my favorite lessons is that great leaders succeed not because they are great, but because they bring out the greatness in others," said business consultant and best-selling author Jon Gordon in an interview with William Parker in 2013. "Once I took the focus off me and focused on making a difference in the lives of others, everything changed."

Teamers get people "on the bus." They create the emotional connection in the workplace and make people feel a sense of personal buy-in on their contribution to the work. They are the people who listen intently to understand concerns and passions about the project. They share all the stories of successes as things progress with the vision. They happily bring people back to the center of why the initiative is essential and bind people together with shared connections. The Teamer remembers everyone's names and the personal details of those on the team that the rest of us forget. He makes us love working with the team and makes work a fun place to be.

Teamers use statements like:

- *We should make sure everyone is on board*
- *We could make this fun*
- *I feel like this could be really good for everyone*

They are very uncomfortable with disharmony on the team. A Teamer's motivation is bringing people closer to those above them and into alignment with the mission or vision.

Are you a Teamer?

- Do you come up with ideas for the group to have fun together, for a happy hour or a potluck lunch?
- Do you float around the office talking to people, not just about work but about people's kids and local sporting events?
- Are you happy and smiling even when things are challenging? Are you the person everyone likes?

- Are you the person that people go to when they want to know what the heck is really going on?
- Do people confide in you first?

If you are working with a Teamer, he will want to know who needs to be in the loop to maintain harmony with your department. He wants to make sure that no one is hurt, ever. He moves about the company communicating with people with the purpose of building trust and camaraderie. He leans toward believing in the positive side of people.

WHY HARDWIRING IS IMPORTANT

A person's hardwiring ties directly into their personal expectations. People at work just assume that others will think the same way when presented with information. But if you are a Visionary, you are going to see business from a totally different perspective than a Teamer. Both perspectives are important, but the expectations are different. Remember, met and exceeded expectations are what creates a positive culture.

Guiding people toward their natural hardwiring allows them to shine their light. You showcase their personal contribution to the team. This reflects positively upon their identity, creating meaning in their work.

By speaking in the person's native hardwiring language, you are able to manage your expectations with all people, not just those in the workplace.

CHAPTER 11

Hardwiring at A Glance

UNDERSTANDING HOW HARDWIRING AND A PERSON'S NATURE GO together gives you clarity in what their motivators are at work. This list is a guideline (not a rule) to help you identify your ecosystem and navigate ideas faster through the pipeline.

POWER ABUSER VISIONARY—THEY THINK THAT THEY ALWAYS KNOW MORE THAN YOU

If the leader is a Power Abuser Visionary, he believes that he knows everything. If you want him to think differently, you have to lead with a fact from his trusted go-to source that supports your headline. Present the points that diverge from his existing way of thinking to create doubt in his mind, and do so with humility, as he likely sees himself as more important than you.

Deliver the goods in short, simple points. Get to the point quickly. Give only enough information for him to connect the dots on his own. Power Abuser Visionaries understand the value of something given to them because they are so in tune with their selfish goals. The Power Abuser Visionary will want to absorb your factual additions to the vision and claim them as his own or pivot to maintain his reputation.

It must be his idea. Do not expect him to show any gratitude and do not wait to hear anything back. You will know if the initiative will move forward when he announces it as his own. Your win was the meeting and the seeding of the problem.

RIP VISIONARY—THEY OVERTHINK

Meeting with an RIP Visionary can drag on timewise. Prepare to be interrupted. RIP Visionaries want to philosophize on all the potential outcomes of what could happen if you address or fail to address the issue.

Think through the probabilities in advance. Your goal is to get a decision before the meeting ends. It is a good idea to prepare three bulleted solutions for him to choose from to avoid wheel spinning—because the wheels *will* spin out of control unless you keep the meeting focused.

Try to present the options early in the meeting, and get a decision as soon as you can, lest he fill the time with futuristic ideas.

SMUGGLER VISIONARIES—THEY PAINT PICTURES THAT MAKE YOU WANT TO JOIN THEM ON THE ADVENTURE

Smugglers who are Visionaries paint pictures that make you want to join them on the adventure. They create the story in your mind on what the future holds and invite you to come along with them. You follow them because you believe in what they are trying to accomplish.

A Smuggler Visionary embraces your ideas to hone the big-picture. You won't have to do anything except directly address how your plan can add to the vision. Smugglers appreciate when new ways of thinking come along to make ideas sharper and more focused.

POWER ABUSER KNOWER—THEY WITHHOLD INFORMATION TO THEIR ADVANTAGE

If you are working with a Power Abuser Knower, they will take all the information that they can suck out of you but not share knowledge in return. They want the information for their own purposes, like when they need to win. They will not let you meet their connections. They want to control how the information flows.

To elicit knowledge from a Power Abuser Knower, pinpoint what you want to know and why. If he sees your reasoning as nonthreatening, he will share. If he perceives it as a threat, you will be tied to the chair with one lightbulb swinging above your head as you are grilled for information.

Also, if he thinks you are asking for the ten-thousand-foot picture, and he doesn't want to give it to you, ask him for a couple of five-thousand-foot answers. Then use your smuggling network to find the other pieces of the puzzle so you can understand the big picture on your own. He is protecting what makes him valuable in his eyes to others—his knowledge. If you have what he has, he believes that he is less valuable to his group.

Finally, know that the notion of reciprocity is not balanced when working with a Power Abuser Knower. You might share a piece of information that is quite valuable to him but get the minimum—only what he is willing to give you in return.

RIP KNOWER—THEY KNOW A LOT OF THINGS THAT AREN'T RELEVANT TO THE INITIATIVE

If you are working with an RIP Knower, he will offer you ten different connections that you can use and will connect you with all of them. He will then want to be briefed on your conversations.

You will not be sure which relationship is the right one for your project. Time will accrue on the project. It is best to engage the RIP Knower when you have a specific request for an introduction. That way the RIP Knower will feel valued, and you will manage your time.

SMUGGLER KNOWER— THEY FILL KNOWLEDGE GAPS

A Smuggler Knower will not sleep until he has the answer for you. Not only does he not want to let you down, but he also takes solving a puzzle as a personal challenge. Smuggler Knowers are adept at finding solutions from other industries. They have networks inside and out, which saves them time in uncovering information.

Smuggler Knowers understand that someone has probably thought of the question before. They just need the time to find the answer.

POWER ABUSER DOER— THEY THINK EVERYTHING IS ON FIRE

I have found that Power Abuser Doers tend to have short tempers and short memories because they are reactive. In their minds, everything is on fire. They are in charge, and you must obey.

If you work for a Power Abuser Doer, he will prioritize your work and give you an official to-do list. He doesn't want you to think. He wants you to execute his vision, which may include taking the knowledge he wanted you to dig for and putting it in a colorful and sexy PowerPoint. He wants to impress the higher-ups with the speed of the tactical progress while setting himself apart from his peers. Remember to speak in the same action terms that he uses and schedule as many meetings as he requests. Updates are essential to him.

Follow through with a recap of your meetings with a Power Abuser Doer to ensure you are managing his expectations. Document when and where all decisions are made and who was responsible for the decision. This extra step might be a total pain, especially if you are hardwired differently. However, this additional action will help you to avoid conflict. If things aren't getting done, the Power Abuser Doer will take it personally. Failure to "do" doesn't reflect positively on his identity as someone who gets it done.

RIP DOER—THEY MANAGE MINUTIAE

If you work with an RIP Doer, he draws up multiple task lists, but nothing is completed because the focus is diffused among projects. These folks are quickly overwhelmed and can shut down.

Distraction is another hallmark of an RIP Doer. These are the folks who flit and flutter around thinking that they are making incredible progress.

The best way to help them is through prioritizing the work to minimize their fears and advance the project.

SMUGGLER DOER—THEY GET IT DONE

When you work with a Smuggler Doer, stand back and prepared to be amazed. The amount of work that these folks get done is just incredible. They can multitask and will think through details that you did not even consider. You can tell them what needs to be done and then forget about it, because you can trust they will see the task through to fulfillment. Do you see why working with Smugglers saves you so much time?

POWER ABUSER TEAMER—THEY WEAVE STORIES TO THEIR ADVANTAGE OR YOUR DISADVANTAGE

Power Abuser Teamers are dangerous people to know. They have no loyalty to anyone. A Power Abuser Teamer's allegiance may change with whoever serves his needs at the time.

He seeds unpleasant information about his enemies, which could be you at some point. His stories have the potential to impact where dollars are allocated.

Never discuss a Power Abuser Teamer's nature with others. That information has the potential to get back to him and create a negative feeling, which he will share with anyone willing to listen. Say nothing at all and keep your cards close to the vest so that this person will not perceive you as a threat.

When you present him with your great idea, he may be defensive about with whom you share information. He will either want to hide the information or want you to share it only with the people he likes. Your project may not go anywhere because of the Power Abuser Teamer's fundamental lack of trust.

RIP TEAMER—THEY SPILL THE BEANS

If you are dealing with an RIP Teamer, you will find that while they are genuinely nice, they just can't help but spill the beans on anything. If there is a surprise birthday party, the RIP Teamer will ask the birthday boy if he is going to the party at 4:00, forgetting it is that person's party. If he knows confidential information about a new product release and is standing next to a competitor on the soccer field, he just can't help but give the guy a "heads up" as to what is coming. The Teamer believes that he is a sincere person trying to help other people. Smugglers know not to share too much with an RIP Teamer—or on the other end, share everything if they want to spread the word.

SMUGGLER TEAMER—THEY GET PEOPLE ON THE BUS

But watch out. When you get a Smuggler Teamer, you can't help but want to do your best because you will not want to let them down. Smuggler Teamers touch you emotionally because they see your contribution to the team as valuable. They believe in you and your potential and tell you so.

HARDWIRING WORKS WITH PEOPLE YOU HAVEN'T MET YET

You can tell how a person is hardwired by understanding how to interpret the words they use on their LinkedIn profile. For instance, if a person is a Visionary, they will use words that describe themselves as visionary, future thinking, etc. on their page. If they are a Doer, they will present a list of accomplishments that are practical and tactical. Knowers list trainings and conferences they have attended and share articles from differing industries (not one industry). Teamers are the folks who offer congratulations and supportive messages and use the words collaboration and teaming to describe themselves.

Smugglers are transparent in their descriptions of who they are on LinkedIn. Power Abusers tend not to list much unless they are in academia, and RIPs use a crazy amount of jargon.

CHAPTER 12

Do You See These Behaviors at Work?

PEOPLE ARE CONSISTENTLY "CONSISTENT" WITH THEIR BEHAVIORS. The sites they use to surf the internet, the channels they watch on TV, the types of books that they read. Think about where you eat, what you order, and who you eat with. Think about your morning routine.

I would make a horrible criminal. My life is one big fat habit, and the police could expect to find me at Target, Kuhn's Grocery, or Bellesario's pizza pretty much any day of the week. Habits are also why behavior change is so difficult. My habitual behaviors represent my inertia. It would require conscious thought to change my patterns. I would have to swim against the current of my default behaviors to do things differently.

As a Smuggler, your objective is to get a Corporate Conformist to change his behavior and adopt your proposed change. Individuals show a high tendency to stick with decisions that keep their inertia intact.

DECISION FATIGUE

In 2011, *The New York Times* published an article titled "Do You Suffer from Decision Fatigue?"* This article referenced the decisions made by a parole board. Prisoners who appeared early in the morning received parole about 70 percent of the time. Those who had court times late in the day were paroled less than 10 percent of the time.

Dr. Roy F. Baumeister, one of the world's most prolific and influential psychologists, discovered that there is a finite store of mental energy allowed daily for exerting self-control.** What that essentially means is that there are only so many "sound" decisions you can make in a day. Things that would have garnered a no in the morning might get a yes in the afternoon.

Decision fatigue resets each day. These decisions aren't limited to work decisions. They are also personal decisions. Have you ever done a great job of sticking to your diet in the morning only to see it fly out the window later in the day?

If you want to advance your idea, observe the patterns of your Corporate Conformist. It might be good to wait for that morning

---

* Tierney, J. (2011, August 21). Do You Suffer From Decision Fatigue? Retrieved from New York Times: http://www.nytimes.com/2011/08/21/magazine/do-you-suffer-from-decision-fatigue.html

** Muraven, Mark; Tice, Dianne; Baumeister, Roy F., Self-Control as Limited Resource: Regulatory Depletion Patterns, Journal of Personality and Social Psychology, 1998, pp.774-789. Retrieved from http://persweb.wabash.edu/facstaff/hortonr/articles%20for%20class/Muraven%20self-regulatoin.pdf

time slot with the boss, or maybe the later time slot, depending on what you are trying to achieve. Knowing about your leader's decision fatigue patterns will teach you the best time to approach him with your opportunities.

DECISIONS AND TIME

People will decide to quit before they start if an idea is too much work. Instant, easy, and pleasurable beats future benefits of the effort.

Why? Because now is certain. The future is uncertain. The instant gratification of a win now means more than the uncertainty of a more significant success later. People who consider a long-term decision might think, "I won't even be working here when this comes to life."

People aren't all that great at linking time and value in a way that they can invest in emotionally. People also envision that they have more time and mental energy to consider a change in the future. As a result, they ignore the future consequences of their decisions today.

When communicating your idea, bring it down to short-term, immediate gratification wins. You make it easy to see success fast moving in the direction that you have envisioned for the project. You don't need to sell the big picture. You want to create multiple successes to build their confidence and investment in the idea.

FOLLOWER OR LEADER?

Agreement to support an idea is like buying stock. The gamble feels as if it has better odds if other people are already on board minimizing risk exposure. We imagine things and people we are familiar with or fond of as better. Familiarity creates the "halo effect." This heuristic sounds like, "Well, he is one of Joe's people, so we should listen to what he has to say." It works the opposite way, too. If someone can't stand your boss, you get the raw end of the stick via affiliation. Use this halo effect to advance your idea.

WRITE DOWN THE REASONS

When a Corporate Conformist tells you yes or no, track the reasons (or excuses) that he gives you. Then, analyze those reasons to determine the pattern. Once you see a pattern, you can test ways around the listed objections. You have created an experiment to find that needle in the haystack. What is the pattern of objections that you must overcome first in your pitches for a new idea?

QUESTIONS TO PROMPT YOU TO OBSERVE BEHAVIORS

To determine the current patterns of behavior—the personal inertia—ask yourself these questions about your Corporate Conformist:

1. What are his behaviors around time? Does he cancel last minute? Does he wing it? Did he read it? Does he say, I saw your email but would like you to explain it to me once again (because he didn't read it at all)?

2. Is he more inclined to say yes in group meetings? One-on-one? Is he more likely to agree if you have a step-by-step process?

3. What are his behaviors when stress hits? Do you observe that he makes ethical decisions all of the time? Some of the time? Does he avoid decisions? When and why? Does he put off meetings the week he meets with his boss? Is he tense or more relaxed after his monthly meeting with the SVP?

4. How does he evaluate opportunities? Does he make emotional decisions on the fly? Does he take time to reach a decision or does he make decisions impulsively? Data or gut feel? If data, which sources mean something to him? How much is enough?

5. Are his peers involved or removed from his decisions? Are there any peers that he doesn't get along with that you need involved in your project? Does he say yes to some people more than others? Do you know why? Who does he listen to for advice?

6. What distracts him? Does he lose interest in initiatives when other "shinier" projects come along, especially plans with a long build cycle? Is he more likely to give you his full attention in the morning or right after lunch?

7. Does he listen with the intent to understand or does he interrupt to tell you all he knows? Where does he get his information?

The answers to these questions offer insight as to how to manage this person and how to "time your asks" to improve your chances of success. Brainstorm ways that you can smuggle around, or align with, his observable patterns for seeking out answers to his questions. Work within his personal inertia.

MATURITY LEVELS VARY BETWEEN INDIVIDUALS

People have distinct levels of emotional maturity. The fear of upsetting others can cause extreme anxiety. The fear of being disliked can bring people to tears.

People have learned behavioral responses to stress. Having the emotional maturity to deal with these stressors isn't a given with age. People act out on these stressors at work in childlike, adolescent, and adult ways. By studying the behaviors, you can determine where force field frictions exist.

THE CHILD BOSS

An example of the behaviors of someone with the maturity of a child includes name calling, yelling at coworkers, and refusing to participate as a team player. They blame others for efforts that go south, just like an only child who doesn't know who drew on the walls.

The behavior is not only obnoxious, but it also dictates that when a Corporate Conformist leader has an outburst, no one can challenge them—especially not minions like you.

Katherine, an accountant and CFO, said:

> *"I work with a CEO of a midsize bond company. An explosive temper and always has to be right, and he is often*

very wrong. I'm the accountant but act as the CFO, but he doesn't know what a CFO does, but whatever. He brought me a box of receipts. I looked inside the box to find receipts from a drug store for STD kits, seedy hotels, not so nice establishments if you will. It doesn't take a genius to figure out what was going on here. I told him that I really couldn't expense them because they aren't business expenses. He hit the roof screaming, 'I own the company! I can do whatever I want! This is bullshit. You had better do your job.'

In the calmest voice, I said, 'Let me look into this. Maybe I'm wrong. I'll let you know tomorrow what I find out.' I wasn't wrong. I just didn't want to deal with his nonsense right there and then when he was throwing a temper tantrum. I printed out the IRS definition of business expenses versus personal expenses. I left it on his desk with the proper items highlighted. Later, I stopped in with an apologetic face and asked him if he still wanted me to process his expenses. He said no.

He had to reach the correct conclusion on his own. Temper tantrum managed."

THE TEEN BOSS

An example of the maturity of a teen is a person willing to do anything to be included socially with his peer group. It is a freshman football player trying his hardest to hang out with the varsity football players. It is, in the simplest terms, the motivation is to fit in and be accepted.

Teens are also ready to shift the blame when the heat is on. Or to hook up with colleagues, because they just can't control themselves in a professional environment.

Jessica, a computer scientist at a multinational tech company, said, *"My employer is a large multinational corporation. It encourages constructive dialogue with a person you have a conflict with before escalating it to management. This woman didn't like what I had to say and leaned over and spoke to me through gritted teeth that she can't stand me and not to ever speak to her again. Shockingly unprofessional. I felt like I was on a middle school playground."*

Corporate Conformists with the maturity of a teen use character attacks as well as social isolation, just like they did in high school.

THE ADULT BOSS

A mature adult-like reaction would be to accept accountability for a project or a relationship that has gone wrong. Adults follow through on commitments and have difficult conversations in person.

Neenah, a staff sergeant in the army, said, *"Oh I make a lot of mistakes. The best thing you can do is to say that you are sorry and that it won't happen again. And then make sure it doesn't happen again."*

We need more adult-like reactions in corporate America, don't you think?

CHAPTER 13

Mental Starting Stalls

IN HORSE RACING, A FLAT RACE IS RUN ON A LEVEL COURSE WITH all horses starting from the same point, the starting stall. Once the horses are in the starting stall, the race is ready to start. The front gates are released simultaneously, allowing all the horses to run hard toward the finish line.

But, there is a part of horse racing that you may not have known. The horses hate the metal starting stall. They get anxious being confined to a space that is just shy of how big they are. But you still need them to be in there to start the race. How is it done?

There are people who manage the horses: the starting stall crew. This starting stall crew takes the time to understand the horses and their patterns of behavior. Rather than forcing a skittish horse into a scary scenario, they introduce the horse to the stall before the race. The point is so that the horse can smell the space and see that it is harmless for themselves. A crew member will walk the horse through with no barriers, and the next time will pause inside the stall, allowing the horse to understand that it is nothing to fear. It is through this patient process that most horses will voluntarily enter the starting stall on their own. The horses have built their confidence.

In a dysfunctional system, you are not a member of the starting stall crew, you ARE the starting stall crew.

In a functional company, you expect people to get on board with your project for the good of the team. You expect the stakeholder "horses" to run to the starting stall on their own.

But you work in a dysfunctional company where there are unrealistic expectations that Corporate Conformists will support your efforts. There is a lot of mental preparation that needs to happen in our stakeholders' minds, just like the horses, before that project has a chance to move forward in the actual "race."

Smugglers discreetly lay a foundation for behavior change just like a starting stall crew, making the race (the project) a priority. Each stakeholder's perspective and motivations are examined. But rather than use a harness with a racing bit to get the horse into the gate, how can a Smugglers prompt the stakeholders to walk into the starting stall willingly?

UNCERTAINTY IS YOUR FRIEND

People do not want to lose the comfort of giving up something certain, even if what they are doing isn't working. The status quo is safer than the "risk" of trying something new; of the uncertain future.

To create the behavior change needed to support your project, you need to make the status quo uncertain for your Corporate Conformist. You need to make the status quo feel unsafe.

For instance, would a horse feel unsafe if it smelled smoke and thought the barn was on fire? That would disrupt the status quo for sure. The horse's behavior would be to kick down the barn door and run away!

People, like horses, don't like uncertainty and threats to what is known and comfortable. If Corporate Conformists aren't uncomfortable, then it isn't a priority. They will stay in the corporate "stable", eating oats, perfectly content with the status quo.

The way you create the "smoke and fire" to prompt behavior change with your Corporate Conformists requires a two-pronged strategy. One that creates uncertainty with the Corporate Conformist *group* and one that creates uncertainty with the *individual*.

GROUP UNCERTAINTY

You can't just create the feelings of uncertainty with one stakeholder. You must create it with the entire internal stakeholder chain.

Why?

Because Corporate Conformists talk to each other. Therefore, the crisis of uncertainty must be seeded with all stakeholders at the same time, so when they do talk to each other, they reinforce the idea that there is uncertainty, that the status quo isn't working, and something needs to be done.

You want the collective hive to adopt the crisis points on their own, fanning the flame and lighting the fire with others. You are tapping into their feelings of being relevant to their group by sharing news. They reinforce your point that there is a problem, and it reflects poorly on the members of the group. Uncertainty about how the status quo reflects on the group's reputation, time, resources, or morale in a negative way is the trigger for behavior change.

People must hear messages several times before they even have a clue of what you are trying to communicate. Repetition creates familiarity. Familiarity leads to comprehension. Comprehension makes it easy for others to share the message. Share the headlines. People who aren't infected by the uncertainty don't need the researched details until they do.

Your group uncertainty headlines might sound like this:

- *We are behind the curve*
- *Our competitors are crushing us*
- *We are paying way too much*
- *It takes us twice as long*
- *We are exposed*
- *The business community is talking badly about us*

Use the headlines that you thoughtfully create, and hit on them again, and again. Use the message discipline that is used on you, by companies and politicians, in reverse, from the minion level. The message needs to be clear enough to be shared easily with others.

As people chit-chat, they use the same exact bullets to efficiently demonstrate that they are in the know on the problem. "Did you know how much money we are wasting on project X? It is embarrassing!" Stay on message and let that headline buzz around the conversation at the water cooler.

People change their behavior to avoid the feelings associated with uncertainty. As a result, you have your horses, the stakeholders, walking to the starting stall all on their own. They are willing to consider your solutions to get out of the state of discomfort.

The back gate is locked once all the stakeholders agree on the correct problem to be solved—the behavior they *collectively* want to change.

When the stakeholders have moved from the status quo to looking for solutions, that is when they are ready to hear about your ideas. They are ready to grab onto solutions to escape these uncomfortable feelings. That solution is your project.

INDIVIDUAL UNCERTAINTY

Now, some of the stakeholders will walk into that starting stall with just the group uncertainty. Others require an extra push.

To do this, use the person's natural hardwiring to create the crisis. Have your message tight and emotionally meaningful for each stakeholder based on what you have observed about their personal motivations. Because you will be hitting their foundation, eroding their confidence in the status quo in their native hardwiring language, you have planted a seed that they will water on their own.

Everyone has their own crisis point where they realize that they have to act and change their behavior.

VISIONARY—VISION SIDE-RAILED

For a Visionary, any threat to the long-term, big-picture vision stresses them out and will move them to positive or negative action. You want the Visionary to contribute their own worry about being wrong in their prediction of the future.

KNOWER—KEPT IN THE DARK

Being blindsided by the unknown, or a missing piece of the puzzle, is devastating to a Knower. They will be rattled that they were caught off guard by their lack of information, and they will double down, diving into more research to see if the information is correct or not. Intrigue him enough about the additional information so that he changes his behavior and hunts for the truth on his own.

DOER—HANDS TIED

Telling a Doer that they aren't allowed to do something makes them feel useless, which is opposite their identity. To tell them they can't do something gives you the opportunity to offer something they can do instead. You want your Doer to find the information to prompt action toward a solution.

TEAMER—IN-PERSON CONFLICT

Teamers who experience personal conflict will face what they hate most—having an uncomfortable conversation with someone else in person. Conflict via technology isn't what will stress out a Teamer. It is eye-to-eye stressors that will get them to change their behavior.

SMUGGLING UNCERTAINTY THROUGH VENDORS

Right now, you probably share facts and research generated from the market to support your arguments. But, that is the status quo.

Smugglers know that a stakeholder has to be influenced by all sides, not just one minion. Having vendors share a story is a way to smuggle uncertainty to a stakeholder without them even knowing that the information is coming from you.

Smuggler vendors are a neutral third party who help you leapfrog over the wall of no to smuggle uncertainty and eventually potential solutions to Smugglers higher up in the food chain. Smuggler vendors fill in knowledge gaps and provide real-time feedback on the degree of uncertainty felt by upper management.

SMUGGLING UNCERTAINTY THROUGH PICTURES

If there is any part of your idea that can be captured in images or infographics, do so. Show, don't tell. A picture is worth a thousand words. Pictures make things much more real for stakeholders, especially when you are trying to seed uncertainty. Images are retained 40 percent more than words delivered face to face.*

Forget about waiting for your marketing department to build you an infographic. Use a company like Fiverr.com. For a couple of bucks, you have what you need to move stakeholders into the starting stall in a day. That is worth the price when you need to communicate fast.

SOLUTION IDENTIFIED BY THE STAKEHOLDERS

Once you have successfully gotten all your stakeholders into the starting stalls, it is time to propose solutions inside of the starting gate for all to consider. You want to take your stakeholders from a state of uncertainty to agreeing to the race of getting out of uncertainty.

People need to be heroes when it comes to their identity. So, let them be heroes by demonstrating their value. Visionaries want to see the future before others. Knowers know the clues that people missed. Doers want to get it done. Teamers want to keep everyone moving along together and keep everyone safe. Power Abusers want to be the #1 hero, and RIPs want to be included, but not with too much effort.

Your idea should be 80 percent baked so that the stakeholders inside of the starting stalls can add their 20 percent to become invested in the project solution. It is essential that you leave

---

* Sibley, A. (2018). 19 Reasons You Should Include Visual Content in Your Marketing. Retrieved from Hubspot: https://blog.hubspot.com/blog/tabid/6307/bid/33423/19-reasons-you-should-include-visual-content-in-your-marketing-data.aspx

this wiggle room because people become personally involved in something that will enhance their identity. Once people have put time into a project, they want to see it through because it satisfies their identity of being a productive worker.

If their idea sucks, it doesn't matter. Incorporate it. You want stakeholders to believe that they are contributing value. You can always pivot down the road. For now, the race is about personal investment. Once a person "runs a lap or two," they are less likely to quit the project.

STAGE GATES

For those of you who aren't in project management, stage gates are an approval system that allow you to continue or quit at different self-created milestones. Stage gates are intended to manage expectations and minimize the fear inherent in risk. Incremental confidence boosts are required to make people comfortable with the small steps toward change. Use stage gates to advance ideas through positive or negative reinforcement of identity. You are building your stakeholders' confidence with each incremental win that results in success.

Some people spend a lot of time making this technique fancy. But you can use a simple PowerPoint template. All stage gates have two elements—time to complete identified tasks and a short-term stopping point to evaluate if you want to continue. Stage gates are easy to create. Let your stakeholders feel what it is like to be their own hero based on how they contribute.

Stage gates are ambiguity destroyers and accountability enforcers. Embrace stage gates. Love them and use them. They build people's confidence.

What motivates people to accept stage gates is the need to escape the state of uncertainty about how the current situation reflects upon their identity—to themselves and others. If getting someone into a starting stall represents a negative reflection of a person's identity, the stage gate represents the opportunity to solidify a new and positive identity, fast. It is the race to bringing the idea to life.

The destination may be exciting. But people realize that "to get from here to there" will be a total pain. "It's too heavy a lift," they'll complain. Many people feel this pain more acutely in the "now." They cannot envision the payoff in the distant and hazy future. It is easier to sell "what we can test today" to make people comfortable with the unknown.

KEEP IT SIMPLE

Simplify your stage gates and make them linear across a timeline (the race), where you can report on momentum versus tasks completed. This allows your stakeholders to make short-term decisions to build confidence and personal investment in the project.

At each stage gate, a project can be allowed to die if it deserves to. A stage gate can also provide an opportunity to get more people on board quickly. If you find that your idea isn't as fantastic as you thought it was, a stage gate gives you some cover as well— the opportunity to say, *"Hey, we may want to nix this idea and try something else, before everyone is too far into the project."*

Your mission is to make Corporate Conformists feel confident in the initiative by using stage gates and reassuring them that their decisions are necessary. This method also allows you to point back to when decisions were made, and by whom, which is useful when working with specific Corporate Conformists who will try to blame you for their poor choices.

ENGAGE A VISIONARY IN THE SOLUTION

For a Visionary, the initial stage-gate decision to move forward could be to gather more specific future information to shape an idea. For instance, a milestone at stage gate one could be, *"By end of year, we will have completed the strategic analysis of the intersecting markets impacting this idea."*

Visionary Corporate Conformists are looking for the big-picture and long-term viability of the project.

ENGAGE A KNOWER IN THE SOLUTION

For a Knower, the stage gate decision could be, *"By June 5th, locate all American vendors capable of producing battery storage solutions for circuit breakers."* Knowers already know a lot. Each deliverable at each stage gate will vary based on what they already know or learn as the project evolves. You can use timelines, but knowledge needed in each phase is what they will be most interested in understanding.

ENGAGE A DOER IN THE SOLUTION

For Doers, a stage-gate decision could be as simple as deciding between a Word doc or a PowerPoint. Doers focus on the details of the moment or the future moment. They may demand a stage gate that is much closer in time—for instance, phase one might be what has been accomplished today, this week, or even this hour.

ENGAGE A TEAMER IN THE SOLUTION

For Teamers, a stage-gate decision could be about who the stakeholders are who need to be included in the project.

Please know that Teamers are the most difficult hardwiring to pin down to stage gates. You might schedule a stage-gate meeting that will be canceled and rescheduled time and again. They want to minimize uncertainty about how others feel about moving forward at each stage gate and won't make it a priority unless there is a crisis. They will then expect to be briefed on what people are saying about the project at that time.

BE PREPARED FOR THE UNEXPECTED

But let me manage your expectations: stage gates are a guideline, not a rule. There will be times where people make emotional decisions or even incorrect decisions that screw up everything. That is where you can use the stage gate to test that bad idea and readjust. Manage your expectations by considering the unknown "unknowns" delivered by the human condition.

Remember, the context of your project changes when different people enter the room. Imagine that you are sitting in a meeting and are close to getting an RIP to make a decision. Then his Power Abuser boss walks into the room. What changes? Everything.

The context of the people in the room changed the power balance. Your decision maker is no longer *the* decision maker, which may change the stage gate process. This is why you think through the needs of all stakeholders; you know how to pivot to another hardwiring when you need to.

One final note. I have used stage gates successfully to bring teams to center. However, I did have one Corporate Conformist who refused to participate in the process. He flat out wouldn't make decisions. He was an RIP and didn't want to be held accountable for anything. If you have someone who does this, just know that the real decision maker is his boss, and that person was never going to participate anyway.

STARTING STALLS AND STAGE GATES USING SMUGGLING

Let's assume your boss is the VP of mergers and acquisition. His job is to develop strategies to identify and evaluate acquisition candidates. These candidates may be competitors or companies that sell complementary products.

Being the minion in this situation, you have found a potential company that you think is a necessary addition to the portfolio. The IP is brilliant, the numbers work well, and you have the chance to scoop them up before anyone else.

Your VP is an RIP Teamer. With your deal, time is of the essence. Wheel spinning by him will sink the opportunity.

Blending your priorities and your VP's using a starting stall is your opportunity to move things along faster. You know what he values—relationships. You also know what causes him angst—conflict in relationships.

To get him into the starting stall, the lever you use is a potential in-person conflict with people. Use emotionally focused words that appeal to his identity to get him into the starting stall. For instance, *"Have you noticed that our pipeline feels like a tortoise in a race? Does it feel that way to you too? Do you think it feels that way to anyone else? John is asking if we have seen anything promising.*

Have you talked with him? He will be so disappointed if we don't find a solution. We meet with him on the fifteenth."

What you have done is seeded doubt that your VP will need to have an in-person meeting to discuss the anemic pipeline with John. Also, you have stressed him out with the information that the pipeline is static and there is nothing to give him.

You then offer up the new company for the portfolio a day later. You say, *"Hey, Joe from another department and I were talking about XYZ company. They could have value for John and for some other folks. Would you like to meet them? I just did a one-pager on them and here are the highlights."* Report on the people you have gone out of your way to talk to in order to minimize his resistance.

You've handed him both the words on a piece of paper, and the validation that someone else thought the idea was a good one. You have given your RIP Teamer a way to get out of feeling uncertain using your proposed initiative to stabilize his feelings. You have also handed him talking points that he can use verbatim for John. You have created a pass-through message.

As you can see, you can use start gates to create pain to get people to admit that the problem is worth solving. You use stage gates to generate the pleasure associated with achieving short-term goals, which creates positive feelings. Each progressive step teaches your stakeholders that they can, in fact, see their enhanced identity and motivates them to reach for it themselves.

CHAPTER 14

Let's See Smuggling in Action

I WAS CONSULTING WITH A GROUP FROM PENN STATE UNIVERSITY. The business community wanted to develop an entrepreneurial ecosystem in State College, PA. There were venture capitalists, incubators, economic development agencies, university representatives, and local politicians on the conference call, all representing their specific interests. They had a shared goal of creating a "Silicon Valley-style" entrepreneurial culture.

What was interesting were the types of questions that individuals asked on the call. Some people would talk about the vision ten years out and the long-term purpose of the ecosystem. Another person would ask a question about what could be done that weekend to get more people involved. Someone else would ask what other models were successful in the country. That statement was followed by an invitation to his home the next time we were in State College. Visionary, Knower, Doer, and Teamer were all on one call competing to be heard.

People set direction with different leadership styles. People have different skill sets and bases of knowledge. Also, people rally teams in diverse ways. One leader can be rah-rah, another a quiet but consistent pusher. This can be great news, or bad news, depending on the team.

This scenario is no different than questions you hear from people in your own departmental meetings. These types of questions are based on people's hardwiring and power nature, not to mention their own unique variables. That static is why meetings can be counterproductive or wildly productive.

WHEN ROLE DOESN'T ALIGN
WITH HARDWIRING

When you have a group of Smugglers and the correct hardwiring for the job, it is heaven. One person does her part, and then another picks up where that person left off and does his part. The work progress is fluid, and everyone is happy because they all contributed their best. Their work holds meaning to them. The team wins together.

But, most people don't get to choose their teams. Further, most of us have no authority to tell people what they can and cannot do. Nor what they need to do to contribute to the success of the group. Smugglers don't have a leader's capability of putting the right people in the right seats.

What happens when you have a Doer who is fabulous at tactics who is promoted to a strategic position? Because the job requires a Visionary outlook, you can predict that this person will not enjoy the work as much as he would a tactical role. You can also predict that he would have more fun focusing on tactical initiatives, like achieving quarterly goals. If he has direct reports, he will naturally gravitate toward the tactical, which other strategic thinkers could perceive as micromanagement. Perhaps a Visionary would have been a better fit for that strategic position.

If it is a Power Abuser with the wrong hardwiring for the role, they may lash out and blame others when they can't play to the best level of performance. If they are an RIP, they will avoid the work. If they are a Smuggler, they will dig in and figure it out but not be nearly as potent as if they were in the right role. When people are promoted to a job where they won't be as effective, their self-confidence is reduced.

People don't just flip a switch and then suddenly think another way. If a person is in a role not aligned with their hardwiring, they stay in a perpetual state of anxiety, increasing their stress if they don't have a manager building their confidence. Or, if they report to a Power Abuser, they are humiliated for not doing a good enough job. If their boss is an RIP, they will not have any support at all.

If you are a person who is not hardwired for the role you're in, you can expect that your performance reviews won't be as impressive, impacting your bonuses and raises.

Seeing people through a Smuggler's lens allows forgiveness when a person isn't naturally hardwired to do their job. You lower your expectations around tasks for which they might not be naturally predisposed. You create opportunities for them to work in the way that they enjoy, allowing them to contribute per their hardwiring. Some people will say that you're compensating for someone else's shortcomings, but what you're doing is more along the lines of readjusting the role to suit a person's strength.

Marianne, a strategic consultant, said:

> *"He (the president of the company) is managing nothing. Our number one need is generating business. But he just spent time himself, in a hundred-person company, drafting a recruitment document to hire new talent. He is focusing on the squeaky wheels of the organization, and not the vision of the future.*
>
> *We created a biz dev strategy and put it on his desk under a header of 'Ideas for 2018.' It was a strategy, along with obvious gaps in the tactical plan, but we wanted it to look really rough. It was a plain jane Word doc because we knew he wouldn't be able to stand it not having nice fonts.*
>
> *We were right, he doctored that thing up with headers and sub headers and then presented it as his own strategy a short time later.*
>
> *We do what we have to do."*

The mental construct of a person's nature and hardwiring is not intended to create force fields. It is not us versus them. When you respect and translate how a person enjoys contributing to the team, you can see where they add value to the project. Because of this, the team is also less likely to cut corners because a person's nature aligns with the tasks. People are inclined to produce excellent work based on having fun in how they want to contribute.

Test this notion of nature and hardwiring in your next meeting. Consider the questions people ask, as well as their answers. Your insights will help you understand their point of view, not just in the meeting, but in all projects moving forward.

Smugglers speak in a coherent language, but we are fluent in Power Abuser, and RIP, which allows us to translate meaning, intention, and common language to ensure that all team members are "heard." This mental construct helps to quickly position yourself and your ideas in a way that will resonate with people, regardless of who walks in the room. It also allows you to translate and bridge people's different hardwiring.

WIDGET, INC.

I'm going to use a fictitious example of a company that we will call Widget, Inc. Joe, the CEO, decides that the company needs a new factory to make more widgets.

Given a hierarchical model, one would expect that the roles of each person would align this way:

- The CEO is a
  - » Rebel
    - » Visionary—He sees the big vision for the future company.
- The factory architect is a
  - » Rebel
    - » Knower—Knows how to solve the design needs based on the CEO's vision.
- The general contractor is a
  - » Rebel
    - » Teamer—Acts as the person to rally the workers and share the vision and the architectural plans.
- The carpenter is a
  - » Rebel
    - » Doer—Gets the job done right and on time.

This alignment is great. The organizational hierarchy aligns with how each person is hardwired. The Visionary and Knower create and shape the vision, and the Doer and Teamer execute and get people on board. Everyone is a go-getter, and they are accountable to the success of the group as a whole.

But that is an ideal scenario. What if you had hardwiring working in this way on the team:

- The CEO is a
  - » Rebel
    - » But he isn't a Visionary. He is a Doer—Wants the job done now. Will start immediately.
- The factory architect is a
  - » Rebel
    - » But he isn't a Knower. He too is a Doer—Wants the job done now. Will start immediately.
- The general contractor is a
  - » Rebel
    - » He isn't a Teamer. He is a Visionary—Needs to understand the big picture.
- The carpenter is a
  - » Rebel
    - » But he isn't a Doer. He is a Knower—Wants to bring the right knowledge to the table.

This team has a more complicated dynamic. The roles and job requirements are not aligned with hardwiring based on the perception of how a hierarchical market is supposed to work. The Visionary and Knower are in tactical roles. The Doer and Teamer are in strategic roles.

They are still Rebels and will figure out how to make things work because of their resilience, but they won't be nearly as effective as they are in the first example.

But reality is more complicated. Communication and intention are taken to another level of confusion when you layer a person's Corporate Conformist nature. For instance:

- CEO
  - » Power Abuser
    - » Doer—I want this factory built in four weeks, and I want to start building it today. Where is the progress report?
- Factory Architect
  - » RIP
    - » Doer—Here is a sketch of the factory. I just guessed at what we needed based on our current factory to save time.
- General Contractor
  - » Power Abuser
    - » Visionary—Wait, why do you want this factory? What is the long-term use of the building now and in the future? I will not start until we know more. You (the CEO and architect) are rushing into things and haven't thought through the consequences of design and function.
- Carpenter
  - » Rebel turned Smuggler
    - » Knower—I have factory building experience from around the country. I just need the blueprints, and I will be able to figure out how to do it.

There will need to be a lot of communication to manage

expectations in this example. You can already predict that there will be tension. The hardwirings are not aligned with the tasks needed to complete the work. These conflicts cost time, resources, and impact the reputation of Widget, Inc.

Any time you have two Power Abusers together, there is a high potential that they will clash. They are both going to want it their way and will not yield because it will make them look weak.

The GC feels he can't progress because the picture in his mind isn't clear, and he won't begin because he is a Power Abuser. He will wait until the CEO comes around to his way of thinking.

Because the CEO title holds the purse strings, he will win. He will either start on his timeline or will drive past or fire the GC for "not being on board." The reputations of both men are now damaged by each other because neither of them can find common ground.

We can also see that the architect is an RIP. She will defer to the Power Abuser CEO and will begin immediately. These two will just start working whether they know what is needed or not. She and the CEO bond on the desire to act and can't understand why the GC can't see that. The Smuggler considers all of this and knows there will be problems with this entire project.

The Smuggler carpenter is a Knower. He sees these potential team tensions before things deploy. Anticipating conflicts allows the Smuggler to use hardwiring language with the team to clarify definitions, bridge communication between individual force fields, and manage expectations for everyone involved in the project. He also designs a plan to allow them all to shine based on their hardwiring.

Is this his job? No. But if he wants to be hired to build this factory, without undue delays and stress, he must proactively defuse the conflicts.

An ounce of prevention is worth a pound of cure.

THERE ARE INDIVIDUAL VARIABLES THAT A SMUGGLER NEEDS TO CONSIDER

On top of that, a Smuggler must uncover who is a headliner, who is a researcher, and any other variable in the mix such as maturity, gender, or generational and cultural differences. (For simplicity in understanding the model, I have not included all variables in this example.)

- CEO
  - » Power Abuser
    - » Doer—I want this factory built in four weeks, and I want to start building it today. Where is the progress report?
      - » Headliner
        - » Teen Maturity—Philanderer
- Factory Architect
  - » RIP
    - » Doer—Here is a sketch of the factory. I just guessed at what we needed based on our current factory to save time.
      - » Headliner
        - » Child Maturity—Has been known to freak out and throw things when people criticize his drawings.
- General Contractor
  - » Power Abuser
    - » Visionary—Wait, why do you want this factory? What is the long-term use of the building now and in the future? I will not start until we know more. He will think

the CEO and architect are rushing into things and haven't thought through the consequences of design and function. And he would be right.

- » Researcher
  - » Greedy—Has a reputation for not paying his contractors on time.
- Carpenter
  - » Smuggler
    - » Knower—I have factory building experience from around the country. I just need the blueprints, and I will be able to figure out how to do it.
      - » Researcher
        - » Over-trusting

THE FACTORY EXAMPLE

In this example, you will take on the role of being the Smuggler Carpenter who is engaged in working with the other three team members.

THE CEO

If we know that the CEO is a Power Abusing Doer who is also a headliner, then he thinks he knows best. He thinks that immediate action is what is needed. He believes this down to his core. Nothing you know is good enough to measure up to what he comprehends. We know he values his opinion over others, fast wins, and tangible results.

Because he is a headliner in a position of power, all your efforts start and stop with him. This is the critical relationship that requires your energy. He has positional power, but he also has the potential to have his short-term decisions cascade in a negative way to the entire team.

He should discover the problem about the lack of long-term strategic thinking on his own. You should loop him back first on why he thinks building the factory is the right solution.

You can state, *"It seems like we need to move fast on this strategic project."* He might say, *"Yes, and the GC is dragging his feet."* Then he adds, *"Have you seen Mary, the new admin? What a hottie."*

This is your opportunity to address his tactical headliner approach. You agree with him. (Just not on the sexist part.)

"I agree with what you said. Getting this built is priority number one. Speed is the only thing we need. You are great at moving things fast, no matter what obstacles come up."

Then, stop talking. Because you are now an ally, there is a high probability that he will come up with his objections to his argument. This might allow you other angles to discuss strategy. If not, you have to push on his hardwiring.

Since he is a Doer, use strong statements or seed questions challenging how speed only works if you are solving the right problem. If things aren't thought through, it will add time to the project. *Time wasted is the crisis to get him into the starting stall.*

"You know, I just thought of something. Our competitor had to close their factory in Pittsburgh four months after they built it. I think their factory was offline for three weeks. How much do you think that cost them?"

Your CEO is a Power Abusing Doer. He focuses on the short term. He will know immediately how much it would cost for three weeks of a plant shutdown. You are entering through the back of the force field. You are smuggling in doubt about rushing to build the project because that is what his competitor did.

Referencing a competitive company stimulates his curiosity because he wants to win. He asks you what you know about the shutdown. This is his first step to the starting stall.

You tell him you have heard rumors, but you will dig in and find out. You have the information already, but you delay because you want him to wonder what happened. You are creating demand for an answer to take him out of his state of uncertainty. The thought of something going wrong and his factory closing is now working in his mind.

You already know the story, but you know you can't tell him what to do. You reach out to your friend who worked at the factory to learn that they closed because the equipment they bought didn't sync with the existing equipment. They had to lay off people just before the holidays because they needed the cashflow to purchase new equipment, which wasn't budgeted for. In the end, the lack of planning added time, money, and a loss of reputation for the company because they had to suspend deliveries.

(If you don't have a buddy working with the competitor, I guarantee that you can find a neutral source explaining the risks of rushing to build a factory.)

You are then able to smuggle this outside information to the CEO, without any comment. The story speaks for itself.

Also, based on his comment about Mary, as well as his reputation of being a philanderer, you know that this is a force field that clashes with yours. You have fundamentally different opinions on such things.

This is not a business ethics issue where you try to guide him to the center. This is a personal ethical issue. In this case, this is the unwritten rule that will not change. He will be a philanderer, with positional power over you. Passing judgment on him will result in a stronger force field between you.

If he brags about it in front of you, it is in your control. You don't need to engage in the conversation or feed his ego with even one comment. Bring the subject back to business. Your lack of reciprocity in this talk will make him question his behavior, at least as it relates to sharing such news with you. By not responding in a way that he expects, you have flexed your force field, sending him a message that his actions aren't okay. You can't change people, but you can change their feelings about things, such as sharing these teenage distractions with you.

You have given the CEO much to consider. When you return, you will find that he did something about the information you provided him. He is a Doer. He has a compulsion to act on all information given to him.

THE ARCHITECT

We know the architect is a Doer RIP headliner. Therefore, we know he wants to get started immediately. But doesn't want the project to fall out of the norm of what he does. We also know the RIP will not venture from the "best practices" he already knows. He doesn't care about power; he cares about minimizing his workload.

He will resist any ideas pushed down to him. He may even sabotage the new way of thinking to guide people back to the old tried and true style he prefers. We know he values his time and getting things done fast and off of his desk.

Here is where smuggling comes in. You think in advance of ideas that could make the project a considerable success. You have your great ideas for what is needed at the ready labeled a, b, and c. All from outside sources that he considers to be the gold standard.

"I agree with what you said about needing to get started. Your drawings are so great it makes things so efficient." You are lowering the force field by reflecting back how he sees himself.

You also know that this architect has a short fuse when it comes to criticism. He has demonstrated the maturity of a child in the past. So, you don't say, *"We need a new and innovative design for the future needs of the factory."* He will perceive it as a judgment.

To get the architect to change his approach, you must create the conditions for him to discover that it is in his best interest to think "creatively." This, however, doesn't happen naturally. He doesn't work to stretch and grow.

You then mention that you saw something that was cool on TV. Robotics and Solar Panels that generate their own energy. Then you say something like, *"I bet the CEO would benefit from a report on that, but I'm not qualified to explain it."*

He may or may not respond to you, but the "undone" task will be dancing in his head.

I would then leave the meeting. When you return, the odds are the Doer will not be able to resist doing. His childlike maturity will work to your advantage—this Doer wants you to give him praise. You took the opportunity to help him over his confidence block by prioritizing his work.

You led him to options which satisfy future growth and business needs. If he just puts in a little bit of extra work on one of these points, you have tapped into his Doer and RIP nature to advance the idea.

You also successfully smuggled a future thinking option on the table for the CEO. You also made the architect feel creative and taught him how to do this on future projects as well.

You build their confidence by giving them a problem that they can solve on their own given their hardwiring. They are both invested personally in the project because you tapped into their confidence.

THE GENERAL CONTRACTOR

As we know, the general contractor is a Visionary, Power Abuser, and researcher. We know he is hip to what is going on in today's market and future market because he researches things and checks the facts out for himself.

His power abusing ways can be brutal to those who challenge him, but you don't question his competence. He wants to get this smartly built so he can grow his reputation and get his money.

He thinks he knows best and probably does. He believes that understanding the big picture is what is needed for all problem-solving activities.

You share with him your belief that the other team members are master tacticians (short-term Doers). You reflect his identity, suggesting that his strategic input is critical to complete this project to everyone's level of satisfaction. Ask him how he thinks the problem should be approached.

He reveals that the worst-case scenario is when he has to get into the weeds managing the times and places of his people. He explains that this adds costs to projects which are always perceived as his error, despite his being clear that he quoted the price based on the original work.

Weeds. Costs. Reputation. We know that he doesn't like messing with the details, he really doesn't like to go over budget, and that when things aren't agreed upon it impacts his reputation. We know that to create harmony, we need to manage the detail work and ensure resources are spent wisely, all so he can get his money fast, while promoting his identity.

You tell him, as a statement, that a starting stall is needed in addition to the stage gates of project management.

The point of the starting stall is to stimulate a discussion between the players on the team. This is for their mutual benefit. If the CEO can start thinking about the future, then that is a win for the General Contractor. If the General Contractor can see the details that are important to the CEO, then there is an opportunity to explain the implications of those detailed decisions.

Each stage gate allows the project to continue to the satisfaction of everyone involved being sure to check on the value and the needs of both.

By offering the general contractor this alternative approach, you ensure that the team, the budget, and the timeline are aligned. The strategic decisions are considered, along with the mitigated risk of cost surprises, providing more certainty of being paid on time.

THE SMUGGLER

As a Smuggler, you evaluate the individuals as well as the force fields that have potential to clash on the team. You can see the issues before they happen and take measures to prevent conflict.

Managing feelings based on expectations can reduce anger and other negative emotions. You already know that there is a high likelihood that the plans will change or be delayed. You will have to be the one to break the news of the delays to either the power abusing CEO or the power abusing contractor. You are the one who knows how to appear subservient to the CEO and GC based on your role of achieving the goal. Is this satisfying their egos? Yes, but in a way, that gets the project completed. And it is in your control.

Take the time to understand the people and their natural ways of teaming over the course of a few meetings. You will have a better chance of getting results once you learn the patterns around how people think.

Let them know that you are not trying to take over their thinking but to create clarity and manage expectations for all.

When you have mastered smuggling, you will look at people differently. The minute they start talking, you will understand power nature and hardwiring and what to do about it.

CHAPTER 15

Imagine Understanding the Opposite Sex

EACH GENDER FRUSTRATES THE OTHER IN REAL LIFE, LET ALONE the workplace.

American culture has a gender issue. American children form a point of view that "girls aren't as smart as boys" by the age of six. Despite girls doing better in school, adults assume that boys have a greater "natural ability." There is an expectation that the boys are smart and that girls aren't as sharp. Even today there is a false belief that men are more intelligent and more capable than women.

To me it is confusing. You would think that in our competitive culture, girls doing better in school, or women producing higher quality work, would make them the "winner."

Why is that not the case?

WORD CHOICE

I researched the differences in word choice used between men and women in business. The research went back to the 1950s where the differences between "manly" men and "ultra-feminine" women were especially stark. The residual effects of how genders communicated and interacted throughout history still survives in how we understand and relate to our world today.

Despite women representing half of the population, there are reasons, outside of power abuse, that cause this disparity in gender equality in business. The male/female invisible unwritten rules are prevalent in our culture.

For example, look at these words:

- Demanding
- A tough cookie
- Giving
- Decisive
- Unbending
- Uncompromising
- Outgoing
- Likable
- Logical

Which words are more likely to be assigned to a wo/man? Which words feel stronger as a business quality?

Words matter. Especially when it comes to how you're "labeled" when you are competing for a promotion. Words in one's mind, as well as what is put in a performance review, "stick" to a person.

It isn't that there aren't "likable" men or "uncompromising" women. There are. The point of the exercise is to show how your brain subconsciously assigns meaning to gender with words. Your mind subconsciously separates what you perceive to be as two groups. These invisible energies and tacit assumptions play into our expectations on who we respect and want to work within the business.

Does your resume use male or female language? Do you think that impacts your opportunities? Words that point to gender or other "diversity" labels allow for tacit assumptions by the receiver of the gender message. This impacts objectivity, both on paper and in person.

NAMES REVEALING YOUR GENDER MATTER

Blogger Nicole Hallberg wrote an article entitled "Working While Female" citing an experiment she ran with her colleague Marty Schneider. Both had starkly different experiences.

To summarize, they switched email signatures for a week. Marty tweeted about his experience:

> "...I'm emailing a client back-and-forth about his resume and he is just being IMPOSSIBLE. Rude, dismissive, ignoring my questions.
>
> I was in hell. Everything I asked or suggested was questioned. Clients I could do in my sleep were condescending.
>
> One asked if I was single."

He ended up explaining the signature switch to the client. Marty told the guy that he was not Nicole. The client treated Marty, a man, in an entirely different way:

"Positive reception, thanking me for suggestions, responds promptly, saying 'great questions!' Became a model client. Note: My technique and advice never changed. The only difference was that I had a man's name now."

Marty was Nicole's boss and now understood why it took Nicole longer to get things done. He continued to tweet about his experience as "Nicole."

"By the time she [Nicole] could get clients to accept that she knew what she was doing, I could get halfway through another client.

For me, this was shocking. For her, she was USED to it. She just figured it was part of her job.

I wasn't any better at the job than she was, I just had this invisible advantage."

Meanwhile, Nicole stated in her blog that she wasn't shocked at all about the results of the experiment. She wrote about her experience on Medium, sharing that, *"I had one of the easiest weeks of my professional life. He...didn't."*

But the last thing that Marty tweeted about was interesting to me. He said, *"I showed the boss, and he didn't buy it. I told him that was fine, but I was never critiquing her speed with clients again."*

You see, the boss's behavior is the real issue. Marty saw the reality of the situation and tried to share the information so that his boss could be aware and do something.

The boss dismissed the notion that there could be sexism from a client. If the boss did believe it, he might have come up with ideas to change the dynamic, taking away the disadvantage that Nicole experienced.

My point is that the boss had options. For instance, he could have had everyone use their initials in emails. He could have measured the numbers and productivity to determine the validity of the argument. At the very least, he could have validated Nicole's experience and showed Marty that he trusted his assessment enough to warrant further investigation. The client was a jerk, yes. But the boss reinforced the gender force field.

He is precisely the reason why we smuggle.

THE IMPACT ON YOUR WIFE, DAUGHTER, FEMALE FRIEND, OR FAVORITE HOLLYWOOD ACTRESS

Women automatically work harder to make up the gender difference when measured against a man. The bottom line is that women have to take more time and effort to overcome invisible, unnamed obstacles. Perhaps that is why white women earn 81 cents on the dollar. African American women earn a paltry 65 cents to a white man's dollar. They fight both gender issues *and* racism inside the office and externally with clients. Latinas are paid 59 cents on the dollar—only 9 cents more than being paid *half* of what a white man makes. Puke.

This intangible sexism impacts our confidence, and we come to believe that we are "less than." We see that "he" is doing better and reason that it must mean that he is doing something superior to us. His success plays upon our insecurities by forcing us to wonder how we are deficient.

Women are behind from the word hello.

SENTENCE STRUCTURE— COMMAND VERSUS REQUEST

It's not just words. It is sentence structure. With sentence structure, men command, and women request. Here is an example differentiating the two.

- Woman—Can you move this table over there, please?
- Man—Move the table there.

Softer questions are designed to help a person shape their point of view and to get others to agree to their solution. Sentences are structured as a form of politeness, of deference, by women. We don't want to be pushy, or too domineering, to men and women alike.

"I just feel that choice A is the right decision, don't you think?" A woman sounds indecisive and like she needs the other person's approval. In fact, what a woman is doing is inviting the other person's input. She wants to get his thoughts on the project to help shape her decision. She also wants to build consensus that it is, in fact, the right decision. It isn't that she won't say, *"This is what we are doing"* but, as a woman, it is in her interests to fit the stereotype of being agreeable and friendly.

However, men don't use questioning as much as they use statements. Statements spoken in male language are designed to either command or are used as a starting point. Statements are a matter of fact. When a man leads with a statement, he will follow with more facts to have you consider his main points, logically. This fits the stereotype of men being commanding and uncompromising.

"I require a 5 percent raise and here are the five reasons why." It is a statement. It now allows him to command the conversation

and provide proof about why he deserves the raise. This forces a person not to focus only on the dollars but to consider the case.

It has also made the boss's job easier, because he will have to go to *his* boss to defend why he is increasing your pay. You gave him everything he needs, in a logical order, to convince another man, or woman, of the merits of the promotion. Because men use this "command" language, they appear to be more confident and deserving of the raise.

Use female lingo when questioning to elicit information and to lower a person's force field. Female language ties another person into the answers emotionally. Use male language when messaging. Male language ties logic to the answers. It can be a matter of fact communication or a directive, i.e., this is an instruction telling you what to do.

EXPRESSIVE LANGUAGE AND CLUES TO IDENTITY

Another difference between men and women is observed in expressive language.

Here is an example of expressive language:

- Woman—I can't believe he said that! (Woo HOO!)
- Man—I can't believe he said that! (What a jerk.)

It is the same sentence delivered in two different ways.

Women express when they are excited about something, such as a significant contract win. She will talk about what it means for the department, how she will get to work on such and such. Her excitement reflects what she values as part of her identity.

Pay attention to what she highlights. These are the trigger points which you can use to attract this woman to your ideas.

Men express how they feel when they are angry. This is usually a clue to their identity and how things aren't jibing with their perception of themselves. Expressive language like this communicates the feelings and attitudes he is experiencing. When a man raises his voice at work, pay attention. You can learn a lot about him, based on the content of the rant. This is an unmet expectation of how he sees himself. You can use the same unmet expectation of his identity to get him to let go of his old behavior to embrace your project. It is the lever that will cause him to act.

DID YOU JUST CALL ME CRAZY?

When a woman lashes out, people will comment that she is acting crazy. She must be on her period because she is nuts. She is overreacting. She can't let it go. She is irrational. She is too emotional. She is insane.

If a man lashes out, people will say he is pissed. He is mad as hell. He is giving him a piece of his mind. He is furious.

There is a tacit assumption that the man's anger is valid with this language, and the woman's anger is invalid. That the man is in control of himself, and the woman is not.

Anger with men and anger with women both result in explosion points. I imagine the sound of a revolver cocking. Click, click, click as the hammer is pulled back.

With a man, an event happens and he "gets pissed." The revolver clicks once. He aims, shoots, and barks loudly about his displeasure, and then he is off to the next thing. His manliness is solidified by his decisive actions.

With a woman, an event happens, and she doesn't react openly. The revolver clicks once, but she doesn't shoot. She suppresses her frustration and lets it go. She should see it from someone else's perspective, after all.

A second event happens. The revolver clicks again. But she bites her tongue and avoids confrontation. She doesn't want to be rude because that isn't ladylike.

The third incident occurs. The revolver clicks a third time. She puts someone else's needs ahead of hers because she was taught to wait.

It continues.

By the time the tenth event rolls around, the woman no longer has a cocked revolver. She has dropped it to arm herself with a one-hundred-pound heavy machine gun like the one from *Who Framed Roger Rabbit* and is ready to unleash the heat at offender of "thing number ten." If you are that tenth person, know that you are the cherry on top of a lot of BS that a woman had to contain that day.

Is she crazy? No. She's pissed—just like a man.

The difference is that she hasn't been able to express her feelings because of the unwritten cultural rules of how women "should act" in American society. Our culture tells her that she is valued when she is self-sacrificing, agreeable, and oh so appreciative of what others do for her.

Women aren't crazy. We've just always been forced to follow the unwritten rules of how to be feminine before we could reveal what we were honestly feeling.

Can a woman choose to express her feelings before the tenth click? Sure, if she is willing to trade what society thinks of her not acting like a "normal" woman.

Could a man understand that there is more going on with a woman than the moment when she lashes out? Sure, if he is willing to take the time to understand the social pressures women must manage on top of any conflict.

The old saying is, "If momma ain't happy, ain't nobody happy." Now that you see what the unwritten rules are in being a woman, make momma happy. Don't add bullets to her animated machine gun.

HOW MEN'S BEHAVIOR CHANGED WOMEN'S BEHAVIOR

In every disenfranchised group, there are reasons the stereotypes exist. Women who are fabulous cooks, who love to shop, who are super moms. But these stereotypes are also false. Feel free to ask anyone about the fire I started in the oven on Christmas day, the last time I was in a mall, or the fact that I never have good "snacks" per the kids who come to my house.

It is the same with the stereotype that women in seats of power are tyrants. There is an automatic fear when you are assigned to work with that "type" of woman. Because of stereotypes about women, a woman may be passed up for a leadership role because she might be "catty" and carry grudges. We know what to expect of a male, but when the person in a position of leadership is a female, the overall situation feels that much more unpredictable.

Women have developed coping mechanisms. We practice social distancing and defeminize ourselves to mitigate the business disadvantage of our gender.

The problem is the way we do it. We put our gender down by saying things like "I'm a career woman, and I'm not like most soccer moms." It is a subconscious (and sometimes conscious) strategy to get ahead.

If a woman passes through a good ol' boy's force field, that woman has learned that her success was due to her doing the complete and total opposite of what was expected of her—for instance, being feminine. What's worse is that men who do see us as different think that we are truthful in our assessment about "those" women.

What perhaps is even more disturbing is that we believe that we are different from other women. When women abandon their feminine nature, and take on mirroring men, it doesn't pave the way for other women to pass through the good ol' boy force field. It strengthens the force field that keeps women out. It reinforces the stereotype of "regular" women being ranked "less than."

Professional men like these "low maintenance" women because they are "like them." They don't have to guard themselves in speech, communication style, or even if they act like a pervert. For women, we are just happy to be a part of the club, so we not only endure the nonsense, we actively encourage men to be unfiltered so that we have a shot to achieve our goals.

The unwritten rule between genders is that competitive and aggressive language is appropriate for men. Men are permitted to swear and talk tough. Women are not. Or at least "should not," given our culture. But to fit in with the guys, we learn to adapt a more masculine way of speaking. Nicole, from the switched email experiment, explained in her article, *"I would also like the record to show that I developed a trucker's mouth and bawdy sense of humor precisely because I've always had to act 'like a man' to be found funny and be accepted in male spaces."*

The women who deploy this tactic and get ahead have created a force field between women, a division of one type of woman being better than the other (or others). Rather than help other women get promoted, there is a fear amongst women of limited seats for those who sit with the boys. The number of women allowed "in" becomes competitive. It is a zero-sum game unless we make sure it isn't.

We are complicit in holding other members of our gender back. We betray our own because it is the only behavior that has worked. If there is a woman who has already penetrated the force field, they may bring along another woman, but only the right kind of woman—another who has defeminized herself.

FEMALE PROFESSIONALS ARE VIEWED AS WOMEN FIRST

To some men, a female employee is seen as a woman first—one like their wife or girlfriend. Not as a peer or potential superior. As much as we want to believe that our work should speak for itself, we realize that we (who are not men) will be filtered by our "gender label," which creates an immediate uneven playing field. For instance, it is assumed if a person says CEO that they are referring to a man. But that same person will use a qualifier if the CEO is a woman—a female CEO.

There are people who, in their private lives, want men to be manly and women to be feminine. Some of this is rooted in our ethnic sub-cultures. Traditional gender roles are expected. People like the status quo, as well as tradition.

Because women aren't conforming to the deferential female cultural norm at the office, assertive and directive women are labeled negatively—by both men and women. Competence and power exhibited by a woman is regarded as not feminine, or not feminine enough. Women who speak "male" don't quite fit in with the boys, or the girls.

Be aware that these gender expectations are imprinted in your colleagues' subconscious. People may not realize when they make gender-based decisions, but they do.

At times, because men see you as a woman first, they assume you view them as a man initially as well. When men make unwanted passes at women in a working context, it too is power abuse—just a different kind.

In this type of situation, a woman's inner self-talk about how to be nice in rejecting advances and not create drama kicks in. Women are valued more when we are pleasant. Men are valued more when they are confident, ambitious, and have a sense of humor. If a woman is not afraid of conflict or doesn't overly praise a man for doing his work, she isn't fitting the stereotype and might be labeled a bitch. We don't want to have a reputation as being difficult because that isn't how we are valued.

When a woman is dealing with a client, the gender expectations are even worse. Clients want to meet with us off-site to "get to know" us. We accept in the hopes that this is a sincere request to advance business. When it turns out the guy is not there for professional reasons, but for his vanity, we endure it and try to cut the meeting short. We want to be "professional" and not hurt the reputation of the company by telling the guy to piss off. We stomach the bad behavior but stay silent because speaking out will impact our professional reputation. Sexism is passively accepted.

Why do we endure it? Because if we complain about it to our boss, that account is reassigned to a man who reaps the benefits of the deal. Inheriting the client means that he gets the work. He also gets the dollars attached to the client (managing budgets or commissions/bonuses) which is a resume line item needed for professional mobility and job security. This neutral male is regarded as a team player while the woman has been tagged as a management "concern" when working with male clients. Senior leaders assume the man is better, given his "progress" in working with an account and his numbers on reports.

The questions women ask themselves are: Is it better to endure sexism and keep my career on track? Or, is it better to speak up about sexism and impede my career progress?

We also endure sexism because of the backlash we receive from our peers. Our concerns are laughed off. *"That's just a dude being a dude. You need to let that go."* The acceptance of bad male behavior by men and women alike makes us feel even more vulnerable, as though we are somehow in the wrong—so we don't say anything.

People who observe sexism and say nothing about it are complicit in keeping the inertia alive. They don't want to rock the cultural norms. Women are forced to stand alone in defending themselves in these situations because there is no direct benefit to an uninvolved party speaking out against these behaviors, and there is a risk to themselves if they do.

But then again, let's consider why. Remember, women don't want to be seen as offended because gender is a professional liability. If you are a man, you are scorned for speaking out against another man because you have betrayed your group. Another man may understand the impropriety and want to do something, just like Eminem did for black culture. Eminem lost fans. What are the penalties if you speak out on behalf of yourself or another woman, and the boss is a sexist?

We end up feeling powerless, and our powerlessness is compounded when men remind us that they will continue to do what they want. We give up and submit to sexual harassment. We have been wronged, and we know it, as do our peers. We feel hopeless.

The only time that anyone seems to take sexism in the workplace seriously is when there is a significant settlement given to a woman in a lawsuit. Unless, of course, that settlement is confidential. Because of confidentiality clauses, the majority of settlements like these are kept secret.

Actively defending yourself against sexism in the workplace equals time wasted—the same time that men gain in their productivity. It is baggage that women carry that men don't have to manage.

So, what are we to do?

We smuggle.

To do that, we have to focus on the behavior of a man acting on the belief that he is talking to a woman versus a professional.

We do that with a purpose: To change their behavior. To achieve that goal, we stay on message that in a business context, women are not there to reflect anything about a man's sexuality. We are there for business.

To alter the status quo, we start with a neutral event. Sharing facts. We must wake up the conscious part of another person's mind.

Whether you are a man or a woman having this conversation, you must lower the force fields of men, who may not realize the challenges that women face. You must speak "female" to drop these force fields, to ensure that this person doesn't feel attacked. You need to crack the headline that all is hunky dory in the way that they work with women.

Create a dialogue to teach the facts about men as a group through storytelling. "My girlfriend Sally was thinking of going to HR because of a guy at her office. This man kept approaching her desk, telling her how much he loved how her outfits looked on her, and then he invited her out for drinks. It made her very uncomfortable."

The man you are talking to might say, "That's just the way guys are. He doesn't mean anything by it," or give some other fill-in-the-blank answer that means the same thing.

It's now time to lower his force field by saying, "You know, we have a great working relationship, so I am comfortable telling you this. I know it wasn't your intent, but what you just said made me uneasy. Can I explain why?"

AFFIRMATION FORCE FIELD

This is your opportunity to talk about why that behavior creeped out your friend, from a female perspective. Explain that when this man approaches and stands in front of her desk, she has to stop her work and engage, whether she wants to or not. She has been conditioned to be nice. She doesn't want to be rude, and say, "I'm working. Go away."

You can explain that mentioning her outfit and how it looks on her is inappropriate. When he asks why, tell him to say this to another man: "Hey Joe, I like your outfit." Guys don't say that kind of thing. When a man looks especially dapper, I have heard other men pay a compliment by saying, "What, do you have an interview today?" Words matter and mean different things to men and women.

What's wrong about that man asking the woman, in a workplace setting, to go out to drinks shouldn't be hard to explain. Drinks have the potential to lead to something sexual. Both genders know that. At times, women are hoping for something else, too. But, in your conversation with your colleague, explain that the sexualized behavior is the exception, not the rule regarding how women want to be treated as professionals at the office.

OFFICE ATTIRE

Ohio Congresswoman Marcy Kaptur suggested that the way some House members dressed invited sexual harassment. *"I saw a member yesterday with her cleavage so deep it was down to the floor, and what I've seen…it's really an invitation."** Her comments signaled outrage among women, as a woman's manner of dress is never an invitation for sexual harassment.

We women accentuate and refute our femininity in different ways of dress. The way we dress has the power to make us feel confident. We know we look good, no different than a guy does in a power suit.

In defense of Congresswoman Kaptur, there are Power Abuser women who use their sexual prowess to their professional advantage. These women see men as a means towards an end. They know exactly what they are doing.

Of course, ladies, you can't have it both ways. If you want to be seen as a professional, stop flirting in the coffee room. If you prefer a resume of your professional accomplishments versus your conquests, stop sleeping with coworkers. It is the latter that people will link to your identity. After the relationship fizzles, the man gets the glory of being manly in other men's eyes. You get the reputation of sleeping your way to the top, a label that neither men nor women approve of, fair or not.

Men, how do you differentiate between a woman who wants to be seen as a professional versus a woman who wants to seduce you at the office? It's simple. You assume that neither of them wants to sleep with you.

The odds are ever in your favor.

---

* McLaughlin, K. (2017, December). 'Cleavage down to the floor… is really an invitation'. Retrieved from The Daily Mail: http://www.dailymail.co.uk/news/article-5178517/Congresswoman-says-clothing-provokes-sexual-harassment.html

WHAT TO DO WHEN A GUY TAKES IT TOO FAR

Every woman has their tolerance level for aggressive men. In my opinion, we do not teach women how to send the strongest of all signals that we are not interested.

Most assaults against women are committed by people they know and trust. This impacts us emotionally because we are taught to be agreeable and nice. There are courses women can buy that explain how to see the warning signs to get out of this situation.

I saw a video by No Means No Worldwide. Their sexual assault program was deployed in Africa and taught both boys and girls how to prevent sexual assault. The prevalence of rape is appalling there. These lessons should be taught to all of us—every age, and both genders.

For women, the first defense is verbal. The program teaches the girls to yell, "NO! NO! NO!" giving voice to the "silent no" that is going on in her head. It is a powerful pattern interrupter. Our intuition has been compromised by what society teaches us. Yelling "No" is in direct contrast to our polite, conditioned response of "no, thanks." It is an in your face, aggressive refusal.

The other part of the program was to teach a boy to act like a strong and protective man and to stop other men from sexually assaulting women. This component plays to a strong man's identity.

Let's translate these methods to corporate America. How can women send a strong message that we are a professional first, not a woman who is interested in pursuing a flirtatious or sexual relationship?

At the same time, how can we teach men that it is creepy when men meet us under the guise of business or put us in situations that compromise how we are valued?

Set expectations with your male friends that they need to remember these lessons. They will, at a minimum, know not to demonstrate these behaviors in front of you. They may also pass along the information to other men, promoting social awareness and preventing a whole lot of discomfort for all.

The goal, ladies, is not to shame a guy or group of guys. The goal isn't to be right and prove your point. Your goal is to change men's behavior moving forward. If you work to purposely and publicly shame a man, you, as a minion, have just created an unpleasant label for yourself and fortified his I'm-not-listening force field. Voicing your concerns without asking for a change in behavior sounds like whining.

We must focus on the specific behavior that we are trying to change with men (and women) at work in order to create value around why they should pay attention, while simultaneously creating a negative reflection of identity for people who demonstrate gender discrimination.

Here are some behaviors you can focus on:

- Men interrupting
- Men ignoring women
- Women not being promoted for not being aggressive
- Conference planners forming all-male panels
- Not being included in 18-holes with the big shots

For my male readers: Please don't interrupt women, and don't let other men interrupt, either. Women don't interrupt because we don't want to be rude. Men interrupt to enforce their identity as a man who talks tough and isn't pushed around by someone he perceives as "less than" him. Explain how identity works, as well as how identity is strengthened to broker more respectful conversations.

SHOCK THE SYSTEM—SPEAK MALE

If you are working with someone who you think is a real jerk in a meeting, I have to encourage you to use my shock sentence that makes people stop in their tracks: "Thank you for your judgment."

Remember, the guy in the meeting doesn't think he is a jerk. He is trying to maintain his identity. Being judgmental is not something people tend to value in themselves. Thanking him for his judgment is a pattern interrupter. You can only bust that bad boy out once, so use it when you need to!

It is confusing enough to interrupt his thought pattern and tirade. He might stumble and say, *"This isn't a judgment..."* where you can then say, *"Great. I'll continue. I expect that you will be professional and let me finish."*

The second sentence sets the expectation that you intend to finish but is also a warning that if he does interrupt you, then he isn't professional. If he interrupts you, it will reflect negatively upon his identity.

CONFERENCES

Men, make sure there are women on your panels speaking with you, or add women if you are the organizer. If you are in business, I guarantee that you can find capable women, as we are more than half of the world population. From a business perspective, you owe it to yourself to see through a woman's lens. It will make you a stronger professional.

It is important to note that men will actively "sell themselves" to be on panels and provide keynotes. Again, men are expected to be confident and aggressive to win those seats. Women need to be invited. We don't want to be seen as pushy or aggressive because we will be labeled negatively.

Should you need help finding fabulous women speakers, please visit innovationwomen.com and genderavenger.com. You will never have to wonder where to find women speakers again. Ladies, get yourself a profile too.

Finally, include the women in golf—they are killer from the ladies' tee box on a par five. If we are better golfers than you, realize that it's not a competition. It's a scramble.

SET REAL TIME EXPECTATIONS

If you think about it, male privilege is a dysfunctional, or at least an imbalanced environment. Dealing with gender issues requires smuggling and tenacity. It takes patience. Consider that the women's suffrage movement lasted one hundred years. We women need to continue their work, starting in the workplace.

Our opportunity is to smuggle value through the male force field intelligently. Incremental wins. Eye on the prize. Penetrate the force field by taking the lessons from the women who have successfully made it "in."

Smuggling requires both masculine (competitive) and feminine (cooperative) language. It is like speaking English and Spanish. Learn to speak both sides of the force and become gender-lingual! Teach everyone about the silent gender issues, like words and cultural expectations.

PAVE THE WAY

Speaking both male and female provides the opportunity to find common ground, dispel different interpretations of words and roles, and to dismiss anything that isn't productive in business communication.

Let's not build force fields with our words and behaviors. The time has come to use our voices to change the gender issues at work. We have daughters who need us to pave the way, and we have sons who we need to teach. It isn't a wish or hope. It is a conscious decision to change the world.

Women, don't diss your gender. Get yourself in and then bring other women along. We need to get it in our heads that more women should be there around us, not that there are limited seats. Nothing will change unless we change. Men have no reason to change unless we hold them to a higher standard, and to do that, they have to be given facts about how their behavior reflects negatively upon their identity.

Stand in your power, and don't let the fire inside you burn any less bright. But, realize that this is why you are one of the groups who have to learn to smuggle the most. We Smugglers need to infiltrate the old way of thinking if we have any hope of changing the negative behaviors.

HOPE FOR THE FUTURE

My daughter Bridget, a Gen Z, transferred to a different high school mid-year in eleventh grade.

She went to her first study hall and sat down in a random seat. There were many available seats in the room, so she just picked one and sat down.

A senior boy walked up wearing a football sweatshirt and said, *"Uh, we have a problem. You are in my seat."* Bridget looked around to see other vacant seats, and said, *"Go get another seat, there are plenty to choose from."* He repeated, *"This is my seat"* in a tone suggesting that he had more power over her. She said, *"Well not anymore."*

The teacher came up and told the boy it was her first day and to buzz off.

The next day the same teacher approached Bridget and said, *"Hey, so that you know there are about five football players who normally sit where you are."* My daughter said, *"Well I guess they will have to find someplace else to sit if I get here first."*

Remember, this was day two at her new school.

I was so proud of her. Namely because I wouldn't have had the courage to do that in a new school. Second, because I was conditioned to defer to boys (self-sacrificing, agreeable, and appreciative after all). Third, because I was taught to defer to adults. In this case, a teacher suggested my daughter defer to the boys.

This gives me hope that my daughter will not only demand equality, but she will also not tolerate any sexual harassment. Know why? She stopped the BS on day one. Wonderful job, Bridget. You are an inspiration to all women.

CHAPTER 16

Smuggled Success

A FEW YEARS AGO, I WAS A CONSULTANT WITH A LARGE HEALTHCARE company. One of my last meetings of the day was with a fellow minion who was building slides for a presentation for our new SVP. As a new employee, he was hosting a town hall meeting to introduce himself and set the vision and tone for his tenure.

My friend told me the content of the presentation. It was the same canned nonsense that the executives had been pushing—the same jive message that the employees made fun of on a daily basis.

I begged him, *"Please do not have him talk about that garbage. We don't need to be told that we need to change for the hundredth time. We need the vision of what senior executives want the company to look like in the future. Not some vague change message."* He said he would try. He was tasked with making the corporate message of "we need to change" as good as it could be. I understood what he was saying. It wasn't his call.

This SVP had circulated an email a week before the town hall meeting to all the employees in his division. It was a heartfelt email. It let employees know that they could share anything they thought could help him. He included a link to his confidential email box.

Based on his professional biography, and the sincerity of his outreach, I had deduced that he was a Rebel Knower. At least I was hoping he was a Rebel. Because I learned that this SVP was going to deliver the same old fluff, I decided to send an email to him. I figured if he was a Knower, he would want to know how to position himself for success. The email is paraphrased here:

> *Dear SVP:*
>
> *Morale is the worst it has been in years.*
>
> *I am coming out of the shadows to tell it to you straight. If you want to start off on the right foot here at the company, appeal to the people inside the organization who get shit done. In a functional business, these people are intrapreneurs. Those awesome folks who have a vision and bring it to life. But we work in a dysfunctional organization. Here at our company, these people who get results are outnumbered by the fearful. These champions of change, who are anti-cronyism, anti-work that doesn't create a result, anti-fear, I call "Smugglers."*
>
> *I realize that you are presenting tomorrow. I respectfully ask that you speak directly to the Smugglers in the room. Don't talk about ambiguous goals. Divert, just slightly, with the mission of inspiring hope to the Smugglers. It is critical to assure these people that they are essential in*

creating a new culture—a transparent and collaborative culture committed to customers.

Making change happen isn't a blissful experience. It is a grinding, protracted battle. Average wins, like a big sale, inked, or an introduction of a new product on the shelves, is not when people like us, who exist in the shadows, celebrate. Our victories are commemorated on the down low, inside the hidden smuggling network.

If you want to achieve success, please, appeal to the Smugglers in the organization. Acknowledge that you know the past few years have been dark for us. But the future is bright because you have a plan where Smugglers of ideas don't have to hide anymore. If you make us believe, you have an army at the ready.

It is still not safe to come out as a Smuggler, but we are hopeful that you create a culture where we are valued.

Best,

N

PS—we are rooting for you

After sending the email, I went home. I was disengaged. I wondered whether I had to abandon working in corporate America and flip burgers to stay sane.

The following morning, I logged on to find a response from this SVP.

Natalie,

Thank you. This was a courageous email and has given me a lot to think about. I am on the side of the "Smugglers." I will do my best to create the conditions where real change flourishes.

(Signed the SVP)

I thought, "Isn't that nice. An actual response from someone who is treating me with respect for the gift that I have brought him."

SMUGGLER GLORY

That morning, we piled into the auditorium. I sat in the farthest corner of the room.

The new SVP, who I had not met before, approached the podium. He was wearing the complete corporate look—blue suit, neutral tie, smart glasses. I had tremendous hope that he would lead with a strong presentation. But, I was doubtful, given past leadership presentations in the dysfunctional culture.

He began:

> *"I appreciate you joining us this morning at our first divisional meeting. I had a presentation prepared that had charts and whatnot. I thought I was buttoned up until 5 PM last night. At 5 PM, I received an email to my confidential inbox, which stopped me in my tracks. I had to rework the entire presentation."*

OMG.

> *"You see, I would like to talk about the elephant in the room. That is that things have been challenging for quite some time here at the company. And for those of you who are trying to champion change, it has been a brutal path. Let me quote directly from the email. 'Those of you who are champions of change, who are anti-cronyism, anti-work that doesn't create a result, and anti-fear.'"*

I took a breath. I was smiling now. The SVP heard my message. He was going to change things!

He continued:

> *"The person who wrote the email went on to say that they are a Smuggler of innovative ideas. I liked that because it is a great name for those of us who are trying to effect change. I want everyone to know that I want you to speak up. Share ideas, because the old way of thinking isn't going to get us where we need to go. Speak up. Smuggle. Please send me your thoughts, if it isn't this forum, to my confidential email and I assure you, I will listen."*

I was gasping in my seat, and my hand involuntarily came up covering my mouth. My eyes grew large, and I was holding my breath. I was thinking, "*Shit!* He outed me—he outed me with my word—Smuggler!"

My smuggling network was peppered throughout the room. A fellow Smuggler in management leaned way back in her seat about fifteen chairs down and one row ahead of me. One eye, finding mine, asking me silently if I was the one who wrote the email. I did the only thing that I could do. I winked.

My mind was spinning. I took a breath. I thought, well, shit. You are accountable, best to own it outright. I listened to the rest of the visionary presentation and believed that things were going to change—even if I was "managed out of the company."

There were a few light questions at the end of the presentation. A fellow Smuggler stood up and said, *"Thank you for acknowledging the struggle. It means so much to those of us doing battle daily."*

The SVP put his hand on his chest, leaned forward and said, *"I am on the side of the Smuggler. I am a Smuggler."*

I sat there relishing in the absolute glory, that as a Smuggler, this SVP has paid me the ultimate Smuggler compliment. He not only embraced the essence of what I was communicating, but he added to it and made it even better than it was. That, my friends, is the ultimate win of a Smuggler working in a dysfunctional environment. Not just someone using the words. Someone who understands the meaning and implication of how Smugglers are scarred, bruised, and beaten. Someone who will try to make the beatings stop. At the very least, someone who will listen to new ideas to move from the dysfunctional status quo to a positive vision of a better future. Someone with positional power who will take action to change the behavior of the Corporate Conformist. The cloud to ground lightning strike.

Simon Simov designed a theory of how movements begin. His theory proposes that the first person following someone with an idea is essential to the development of a movement. The follower gives credibility to the initiator and their vision. Others follow the first follower. I was the initiator (Smuggler), and my first follower made it safe for others to join in our smuggling efforts. Together we built a smuggling army that was at the ready to support the new senior vice president in our dysfunctional culture.

That smuggling army now had a general giving a speech about the value of our smuggling efforts and why they are critical to creating change inside of the organization. The general and the smuggling army became two energy sources generating enough energy from either side to form a connection. We transferred knowledge efficiently and succinctly, making the entire circuit work.

When the SVP stood in front of us, in his commanding position, stating that it was okay to come out of the shadows and do our thing, it was a moment of such joy. Such satisfaction. The good guys finally had a coherent champion to fight the dark shadows of stagnation in the organization.

The SVP was now leading the smuggling movement. It was the crowning jewel in smuggling around inertia and Corporate Conformists. We smuggled behavior change in the culture of the company! People were unafraid to speak up knowing that the SVP had their back. It set him off on the right foot as a champion of the employees and leader of positive change.

When I went back to my desk, my entire department stood staring at me. I admitted that I wrote the not-so-confidential-email and was met with both cheers and wide eyes. Later, an Executive Vice President sent me an email, saying that what I did took courage. Yup. Everyone knew it was me.

I left the office in a blaze of glory that day. Using the tactics in this book, I smuggled a critical problem to an SVP in a few short paragraphs to positively influence the culture of my organization.

Amazingly, my boss decided to keep me. All he did was chuckle.

CHAPTER 17

You. Smuggler.

AROUND HALLOWEEN, I SAW AN INTERNET MEME OF FIVE FULL-bodied skeletons standing in a row. They were all the standard version of what you would expect a skeleton to look like. The text beneath the picture asked which skeleton was the boss, worker, rich, poor, winner, loser, and other ways that people measure themselves against others. The gist was that we are all the same. It is the meaning we apply in our world that creates these artificial divides. People protect their identity, based on these divisions, at all costs. Even if doing so means hurting others.

If ethics is the difference between good and bad behavior, how can putting people down by beating them at all costs be moral? How can putting profits over people be moral? We cannot let this negativity run the show. We all have ways to contribute to the success of our company.

We all have only one life to live on earth. We have the choice of encouraging others to do the right thing or passively stand by and watch them make self-serving decisions that impact the emotional health of others. We can't allow profits to supersede ethical lapses and selfish behavior.

How do we smuggle morality and cooperation back into the workplace? How do we make goodness the desired identity that people want? How do we even take our tiny little work bubble and create harmony where people get along and work together?

Through smuggling.

It is our responsibility to make sure other people aren't damaged by any dysfunctional system. It is our duty to lead the way, regardless of our title and position, to direct our companies to a cooperative mindset.

The way to transform the imbalance is to infect the system with ethics, positivity, and openness, creating a contagion of good. Smugglers lower force fields to promote a new way of thinking that people embrace on their own, transforming the company from what is, to what it will become.

SMUGGLERS TAILOR VALUE AND SMUGGLE HOPE

When you are confident, you are empowered, and your positive energy is felt by others. You are in a position to help support another person's identity. When people feel respected, it minimizes the friction between them and others and drives positive results for all. At times, you may need to detract from a person's identity to create some doubts, in order to turn their behavior in a cooperative direction. But, at the end of the road, you are helping people become the version of their best self.

When you are ready to drive change, focus on the solution—the behaviors you would like to see in the future—not the existing behaviors of today. Use the competition mindset to your advantage. Position your initiatives in a way that offers the opportunity to increase a person's "rank."

You will always engage laziness, power abuse, and groupism. These are mind-to-mind battles in a lifetime war that needs a champion, in and out of the office. Guess what, Smuggler. You're the champion. You are going to have to smuggle the desired behavior changes. In a dysfunctional environment, no one else will.

Expect that things are not going to change overnight. Smuggling isn't a one and done. It is a practice. Demonstrating the vigilance to snuff out dysfunction is a long-term strategy. It takes one conversation at a time to drive change.

CONTROL WHAT IS IN YOUR CONTROL

Choose your battles. Don't waste time on unwritten rules that are out of your sphere of control. You are only absorbing negative energy if you do so.

Be alert for opportunities to advance your idea. Time will eventually show you the way—because there is always a way.

Sun Tzu said, *"He who knows when he can fight and when he cannot will be victorious."* Weigh the effort required to spread the cure against the costs of the damage to yourself. Be smart. There are sprints to advance your ideas but ride the glacier when you need to.

CELEBRATE AND MEMORIALIZE YOUR WINS

Kevin, an innovation consultant, told me how he created positivity inside of his dysfunctional workplace:

> *"I worked on a great team with a horrible leader. It was a his-way-or-the-highway kind of person. He would never believe our recommendations. If I were Einstein, he wouldn't have believed me.*
>
> *My team made it a game to use each meeting as a place to hammer on one point of our research. Just one solitary point.*
>
> *We tag-teamed to do this. When we got him to accept that there was a potential fact from our recommendation that was valid, we would celebrate by creating a 'pennant,' a Post-it note on a pencil with the word 'win' written on it.*
>
> *That stupid pencil represented that we were moving forward. An inch at a time, but still forward. The pencil made it easier to come to work, actually. It was no longer about the work. We wanted to win that Post-it note.*
>
> *We expected to fail. And we did. But when we won just one tiny point, we were thrilled. Ridiculous, right? It forced us to sharpen our game. OUR game. We wanted the pennant.*
>
> *We had a lot of laughs. He still expected the BAU work, which we did. But we clawed our way back to fun at work, bringing all of our team out of the sense of dreading work each day."*

In a dysfunctional culture, the smallest of wins should be celebrated with incredible glory. If there is a lack of acknowledgment from Corporate Conformists, create your own methods to recognize your accomplishments. Noticing your small rung wins boosts your confidence. These rungs of the confidence ladder that you have climbed are milestones that should be acknowledged. (My team used to play the Benny Hill theme song for small wins. Incidentally, typing that just made me laugh out loud. We made the toxicity funny, to help us to survive!)

Keep a list of all you have accomplished and return to it when the going gets tough. Decide to achieve just one thing in a day. Envision it as a tiny rung and come up with options so you can climb it no matter what.

When you redefine your expectations, this creates a massive shift in your thinking. You are changing your expectations from being a victim to expecting that your new smuggling lens will make work meaningful. You expect to change your behavior to thrive. You are empowered.

Smuggling redefines your purpose at work. Smuggling becomes your primary purpose in a dysfunctional environment and bringing your projects to life becomes secondary. You are focusing on the game that you have created inside of their game. Your new win is the lowering of the force fields. Advancing initiatives happens naturally as a result of these primary efforts. Whether you see smuggling as an experiment, an obstacle course, or a method that contributes to your personal growth, you are focused on harvesting the results.

HOW TO SMUGGLE GOODNESS AS THE DESIRABLE IDENTITY

Can collaboration work anymore when American culture has conditioned us to be so competitive?

Yes. It can.

Build your Smuggler network. Find each other, not just in your company, but in other industries, and create movements around the forces of cooperation and morality. Cooperation leads to feelings of connectedness and engagement. You feel better when you work with people versus against them. You bond with others when you recognize each other's value. Your self-esteem is not impacted when you pull people together. Shame doesn't exist inside cooperation and ethics. Productivity improves when you work together and suffers when gains are selfish.

Joe, an M&A Vice President, told me how his company embraced a cooperative culture versus a competitive one:

> "I work for a large Japanese company where the culture is very different than American culture. They operate under the premise of 'we' versus the American premise of 'me.' One of the unwritten rules that I learned was that everything that they do has to be in harmony and balance.
>
> For example, I showed them the 'hockey stick revenue curve' that you see in investment growth opportunities and market share potential. The profit potential for our division was great, based on American standards.
>
> However, the deal was scuttled, because I didn't understand the Japanese unwritten rules of harmony and balance. The executives didn't think the deal was fair in cannibalizing the market share of a sister company.
>
> Here in the U.S. we would have said, 'Well that is the other company's problem.' But in Japan, the unwritten culture of 'we' was much more important than profits. I was looking at it from only our company perspective. They were looking at it from the entire portfolio of the global 'we.'"

I understand that Japan has an entirely different culture. I cite this example because Japan has the third largest economy behind the US and China. Apparently, you can have a healthy economy and a cooperative culture, among other beautiful things, like a healthier and longer life expectancy.*

THE PERSON WHO WILL CHANGE EVERYTHING

Your job isn't just the work defined in your job title. Your work is so much more important than that. You ARE the person who transitions the company from the status quo to the new. Rebels:

- Create an underground resistance to the "same old same old"
- Minimize the fear of the new
- Seed thoughts of hope
- Make new ideas popular, with a smile and encouragement that it's cool to back the idea
- Tell the right part of the story to the right person at the right time
- Give unconditionally in an un-giving culture
- Collaborate with those who will collaborate, and team together to advance solutions
- Are willing to lower our own force field and be vulnerable and admit when we don't know the answers
- Are convinced that what we bring to the table will

---

* World Happiness Report. (2017). Retrieved from World Happiness Report: http://worldhappiness.report

make a significant impact on the business and for the good of the world.

You are the captain of your ship regardless of what drama is circulating around you. If you are still looking for that hero who can improve your sad situation at work, look in the mirror. You will feel less stressed now that you have cleared the fog and put color to the invisible forces around you.

Martin Luther King said, *"The arc of the moral universe is long, but it bends toward justice."* While I agree with Dr. King's statement, in my opinion, justice is only possible because Smugglers bend the arc themselves.

Smugglers are the warriors with scars that only other Smugglers can see. But now, we have been given the gift of sight—of being able to see the invisible forces working against our efforts to change things for the better. Now that we see what the obstacles are, we can walk around them and advance our ideas in any kind of workplace.

You are not alone Smuggler. And you can change the world.

Works Cited

Albin-Lackey, C. (2011, 02 01). *Papua New Guinea: Serious Abuses at Barrick Gold Mine.* Retrieved from Human Rights Watch: https://www.hrw.org/news/2011/02/01/papua-new-guinea-serious-abuses-barrick-gold-mine

Amen, D. (Retrieved 2018). *How to Develop Your Own Internal Anteater to Eradicate Automatic Negative Thoughts.* Retrieved from American Holistic Health Association: https://ahha.org/selfhelp-articles/ant-therapy/

Bacon, T. (2011). The Morality of Power. In T. Bacon, *The Elements of Power: Lessons on Leadership and Influence* (p. 305). AMACOM Books. Retrieved from Power and Influence: http://www.theelementsofpower.com/power-and-influence-blog/the-morality-of-power/

Barnhart, T. (2010, January 9). *Thinking Errors Defined.* Retrieved from Corrections: http://www.corrections.com/news/article/23237-thinking-errors-defined

Bebchuk, L., & Fried, J. (2002). Power, Rent Extraction, and Executive Compensation. *CESifo Forum,* 6. Retrieved from http://www.law.harvard.edu/faculty/jfried/Power_Rent_Extraction.pdf

Bebchuk, L., Fried, J., & Walker, J. (2002, June). *Managerial Power and Rent Extaction In the Design of Executive Compensation.* Retrieved from University of Chicago Law Review.

Bernstein, A. (2016, Sep 6). *Whom to Vote For? Employees Tend To Follow Their Leader.* Retrieved from New York Times: https://www.nytimes.com/2016/09/06/business/dealbook/whom-to-vote-for-employees-tend-to-follow-their-leader.html

Bivens, J., & Mishel, L. (2015, September 2). *Understanding the Historic Divergence Between Productivity and a Typical Workers Pay.* Retrieved from Economic Policy Institute: http://www.epi.org/publication/understanding-the-historic-divergence-between-productivity-and-a-typical-workers-pay-why-it-matters-and-why-its-real/

Blanding, M. (2015, January). *Workplace Stress Responsible For Up To $190B In Annual U.S. Healthcare Costs.* Retrieved from Forbes: https://www.forbes.com/sites/hbsworkingknowledge/2015/01/26/workplace-stress-responsible-for-up-to-190-billion-in-annual-u-s-heathcare-costs/#3bddb717235a

Bloom, S. (2000). When Victims Turn Into Bullies. *Psychotherapy Review,* 59-60. Retrieved from http://www.sanctuaryweb.com/Portals/0/Bloom%20Pubs/2000%20Bloom%20Email%20When%20Victims%20Turn%20Into%20Bullies.pdf

Buss, D., Gomes, M., & Lauterbach, K. (1987, June). Tactics of manipulation. *Journal of Personality and Social*

Psychology. Retrieved from The National Center for Biotechnology Information: https://www.ncbi.nlm.nih.gov/pubmed/3598864

Carreyrou, J. (2016, November 18). *Theranos Whistleblower Shook the Company—And His Family.* Retrieved from Wall Street Journal: https://www.wsj.com/articles/theranos-whistleblower-shook-the-companyand-his-family-1479335963

Carucci, R. (2016, December 16). *Why Ethical People Make Unethical Choices.* Retrieved from Harvard Business Review: https://hbr.org/2016/12/why-ethical-people-make-unethical-choices

Chira, S. (2017, June 14). *The Universal Phenomenon of Men Interrupting Women.* Retrieved from New York Times: https://www.nytimes.com/2017/06/14/business/women-sexism-work-huffington-kamala-harris.html

Chua, R., & Zou, X. (2009). The Devil Wears Prada? Effects of Exposure to Luxury Goods on Cognition and Decision Making. *Harvard Business School - Working Paper* . Boston, MA, USA. Retrieved from Harvard Business School: http://www.hbs.edu/faculty/Publication%20Files/10-034.pdf

Chun, S. (2014, Feb 14). *Are We Born With A Moral Core? The Baby Lab Says "Yes".* Retrieved from CNN.com: http://www.cnn.com/2014/02/12/us/baby-lab-morals-ac360/index.html

Courtright, S., Gardner, R., Smith, T., McCormick, B., & Colbert, A. (2013). My Family Made Me Do It: A Cross-Domain, Self-Regulatory Perspective on Antecedents to Abusive Supervision. *Academy of Management Journal*, 55.

Denning, S. (2011, November 28). *The Dumbest Idea In The World: Maximizing Shareholder Value.* Retrieved from Forbes: https://www.forbes.com/sites/stevedenning/2011/11/28/

maximizing-shareholder-value-the-dumbest-idea-in-the-world/#654ab9182287

Denning, S. (2014, August 18). *How CEOs Became Takers, Not Makers*. Retrieved from Forbes: https://www.forbes.com/sites/stevedenning/2014/08/18/hbr-how-ceos-became-takers-not-makers/#151354d69509

Diamond, B. (2015, October 10). *The White Man in That Photo*. Retrieved from Films For Action: http://www.filmsforaction.org/articles/the-white-man-in-that-photo/?utm_medium=google

Egan, M. (2016, September 21). *I called the Wells Fargo ethics line and was fired*. Retrieved from CNN: http://money.cnn.com/2016/09/21/investing/wells-fargo-fired-workers-retaliation-fake-accounts/index.html

Fiegerman, S. (2016, July 28). *Elon Musk's Push for Autopilot Unnerves Some Tesla Employees*. Retrieved from CNN: http://money.cnn.com/2016/07/28/technology/elon-musk-tesla-autopilot/index.html

Flanagan, M. (2006, October 10). *'Tell your kids about Peter Norman'*. Retrieved from The Age: http://www.theage.com.au/news/national/tell-your-kids-about-peter-norman/2006/10/09/1160246071527.html

Fowler, T. (2015, January 19). *High School Basketball Coach Suspended After His Team Crushes Another 161-2*. Retrieved from People: http://people.com/celebrity/high-school-basketball-coach-suspended-after-his-team-crushes-another-161-2/

Gholipour, A., Sanjari, S., Bod, M., & Kozekanan, S. (2011, June). *Organization Bullying and Women Stress in Workplace*. Retrieved from International Journal of Business and Management: file:///C:/Users/natal/Downloads/10845-32524-1-PB.pdf

Gross, T. (2017, December 20). *A Filmmaker's Quest for a Quiet Family Portrait is Pierced by Unforeseen Trauma*. Retrieved from NPR: https://www.npr.org/2017/12/20/572238985/a-filmmakers-quest-for-a-quiet-family-portrait-is-pierced-by-unforeseen-trauma

Guillebeau, C. (2010). *The Art of Non-Conformity.* Penguin Group.

Gutsche, J. (2015). *Better and Faster.* Crown Publishing.

Hagy, J. (2015). *The Art of War Visualized.* Workman Publishing Company.

Holder, T. (2018). Fox News will sue me for speaking out today. (B. Stelter , Interviewer) CNN. Retrieved from http://www.cnn.com/videos/us/2017/12/17/former-fox-contributor-tamara-holder-full-reliable-intv.cnn

Holiday, R. (2014). *The Obstacle Is the Way.* Penguin.

Hwang, V., & Horowitt, G. (2012). *The Rainforest.* Regenwald.

Jarvis, C. (2016, August 10). Chief Epidemiologist Resigns as Fight Over Well Water Safety Escalates. *News & Observer*, p. 2.

Jones, M. (2005, January 3). *The Politics of Failure: Workplace Politics and Poor Performance.* Retrieved from International Institute of Management: https://www.iim-edu.org/thinktank/papers/dysfunctional-leadership-dysfunctional-organizations-paper/index.htm

Jones, M. (2017, May 8). *All Extremely Confident People Give Up These 13 Habits.* Retrieved from Inc: https://www.inc.com/matthew-jones/13-things-you-should-immediately-give-up-if-you-want-astonishing-confidence.html

Kelley, C. (2017, October 11). *Trump-Supporting Eminem Fans Express Outrage on Twitter Over Rapper's Anti-Trump Freestyle.* Retrieved from Billboard: https://www.billboard.com/articles/news/politics/7997498/eminem-trump-freestyle-fan-supporters-twitter

Kohn, A. (2016, August 27). *The Case Against Competition.* Retrieved from Alfie Kohn: http://www.alfiekohn.org/article/case-competition/

Konnikova, M. (2016, July 30). *What Makes People Feel Upbeat at Work*. Retrieved from New Yorker: https://www.newyorker.com/science/maria-konnikova/what-makes-people-feel-upbeat-at-work

Koster, R. (2013, April 16). *Playing With "Game"*. Retrieved from Raph Koster's Website: https://www.raphkoster.com/2013/04/16/playing-with-game/

Kroft, S. (2007, November 30). *Will Smith My Work Ethic is Sickening*. Retrieved from 60 Minutes: https://www.cbsnews.com/news/will-smith-my-work-ethic-is-sickening/

Landrum, S. (2016, April 4). *The Physical Effects of Having a Terrible Job*. Retrieved from Career Builder: https://www.careerbuilder.com/advice/the-physical-effects-of-having-a-terrible-job

Lempiala, T. (2011, March 8). *Corporate Smugglers: Championing Ideas Under the Radar*. Retrieved from Fast Company: https://www.fastcompany.com/1736968/corporate-smugglers-championing-ideas-under-radar

Lipman, V. (2015, April). *The Disturbing Link Between Psychopathy And Leadership*. Retrieved from Forbes: https://www.forbes.com/sites/victorlipman/2013/04/25/the-disturbing-link-between-psychopathy-and-leadership/#4544e1414104

Looting Stars. (2009, June 29). Retrieved from The Economist: http://www.economist.com/node/13035696

Lutgen-Sandvik, P. (December 2006). Take this Job and...: Quitting and Other Forms of Resistance to Workplace Bullying. *Communication Monographs*, pp. 406-433.

Lyell, C. (2013, January 19). *Dopomine Profile: Why Power/Money/Esteem Addicts Are More Dangerous Than Junkies*. Retrieved from Dopamine Project: http://dopamineproject.org/2013/01/why-power-money-and-esteem-addicts-are-more-dangerous-than-junkies/

Marx Hubbard, B. (January 27, 2015). Conscious Evolution: Awakening the Power of Our Social Potential. In B. Marx Hubbard, *Conscious Evolution: Awakening the Power of Our Social Potential* (p. 296). New World Library.

McChesney, F. (1987). Rent Extraction and Rent Creation In The Economic Theory of Regulation. *HeinOnline*, 16 J. Legal Stud. 101 1987.

McGovern, M. (2012, June 21). *How long does one bad experience last in a customer's mind?* Retrieved from Customer Experience Insight: http://www.customerexperienceinsight.com/how-long-does-a-bad-experience-last-in-a-customers-mind/

McIntyre, M. (2005). *Secrets to Winning at Office Politics.* St. Martin's Press.

McLaughlin, K. (2017, December). *'Cleavage down to the floor… is really an invitation'.* Retrieved from The Daily Mail: http://www.dailymail.co.uk/news/article-5178517/Congresswoman-says-clothing-provokes-sexual-harassment.html

McLean, B. (2017, Summer). *Vanity Fair.* Retrieved from How Wells Fargo's Cutthroat Corporate Culture Allegedly Drove Bankers To Fraud: https://www.vanityfair.com/news/2017/05/wells-fargo-corporate-culture-fraud

Mehta, J., & Winship, C. (n.d.). *Moral Power.* Retrieved from Harvard.edu: https://scholar.harvard.edu/files/cwinship/files/moral_power--final_1.pdf

Mishel, L., & Schieder, J. (2016, July 13). *CEO Compensation Grew Faster Than The Wages of The Top .1 Percent and the Stock Market.* Retrieved from Economic Policy Institute: http://www.epi.org/publication/ceo-compensation-grew-faster-than-the-wages-of-the-top-0-1-percent-and-the-stock-market/

Mishel, L., & Schieder, J. (2016, July 12). *Stock market headwinds meant less generous year for some CEOs.* Retrieved from

Economic Policy Institute: http://www.epi.org/publication/ceo-and-worker-pay-in-2015/

Muller, M. (2015, August 4). *Office Beasts: Venomous Employees a 10 Billion Problem in Germany.* Retrieved from Spiegel: http://www.spiegel.de/international/business/toxic-workers-a-10-billion-problem-in-germany-a-1046663.html

Nacke, L. (2014, September 12). *The formal systems of games and game design atoms.* Retrieved from The Acagamic: http://www.acagamic.com/courses/infr1330-2014/the-formal-systems-of-games-and-game-design-atoms/

Namie, R., & Namie, G. (2016, Aug 29). *What Individuals Can Do When Bullied At Work.* Retrieved from Workplace Bullying: http://www.workplacebullying.org/individuals/solutions/wbi-action-plan/

Namie, R., & Namie, G. (2018). *From Bullied to Bully Proof.* Retrieved from Workplace Bullying: http://www.workplacebullying.org/individuals/solutions/wbi-action-plan/

Nelson, A. (2015, July 15). *10 Things Pope Francis Said That May Signal the Dark Side's Demise.* Retrieved from Conscious Life News: https://consciouslifenews.com/10-pope-francis-signal-dark-sides-demise-2/1190940/

Ni, P. (2006). *How to Communicate Effectively and Handle Difficult People.* Retrieved from Ni Preston: http://www.nipreston.com/publications/excerpts/How_to_Handle_FINAL_2006-SAMPLE.pdf

Ni, P. (2015, October 11). *14 Signs of Psychological and Emotional Manipulation.* Retrieved from Psychology Today: https://www.psychologytoday.com/blog/communication-success/201510/14-signs-psychological-and-emotional-manipulation

Oliver, V. (2008). *Bad Bosses, Crazy Coworkers, and Other Office Idiots.* Sourcebooks.

Phipps, M., & Gautrey, C. (2005). *21 Dirty Tricks At Work.* Capstone Publishing.

Police Deployment, Enga Province, Papua New Guinea. (2009, June). Retrieved from Barrick Gold Corporation: http://www.barrick.com/operations/porgera/default.aspx

Polk, S. (2014, January 18). *For the Love of Money.* Retrieved from New York Times: https://www.nytimes.com/2014/01/19/opinion/sunday/for-the-love-of-money.html

Power Really Does Corrupt As Scientists Cliam. It's As Addicitve As Cocaine. (2012, April). Retrieved from Daily Mail: http://www.dailymail.co.uk/news/article-2136547/Power-really-does-corrupt-scientists-claim-addictive-cocaine.html

Pozin, I. (2016, July 28). *Top 10 Reasons People Hate Their Job (And You May Hate Yours).* Retrieved from Inc: https://www.inc.com/ilya-pozin/top-10-reasons-people-hate-their-job-and-you-may-hate-yours.html

Prosser, D. (2015). *Thirteeners.* Greenleaf Book Group Press.

Pullella, P. (2016, Aug 2). *Pope Orders Study of Women's Role In Early Church, Cheering Equality Campaigners.* Retrieved from Rueters: https://in.reuters.com/article/pope-women/pope-orders-study-of-womens-role-in-early-church-cheering-equality-campaigners-idINKCN10D19Z

Radford, T. (2003, November). *The King of the Pharaohs.* Retrieved from The Guardian: https://www.theguardian.com/education/2003/nov/27/research.highereducation

Raven, B. (2008). The Bases of Power and the Power/Interaction. *Analyses of Social Issues and Public Policy, Vol. 8, No. 1,* 1-22.

Raven, B. (2008). The Bases of Power and the Power/Interaction Model of Interpersonal Influence. *The Society for the Psychological Study of Social Issues,* 22.

Redman Reacts To Eminem's Freestyle: "He Used His Platform As A White Artist To Stand Up For US!". (2017, October 19).

Retrieved from BET Networks: https://www.youtube.com/watch?v=wo_GLkvRSis

Re-settlement of people living near a large PNG gold mine has to be affordable - Governor. (2011, 10 18). Retrieved from Radio New Zealand: http://www.radionz.co.nz/international/pacific-news/200271/re-settlement-of-people-living-near-a-large-png-gold-mine-has-to-be-affordable-governor

Robinson, E. (2016, 09 05). *The Ugliest, Most Appalling Spectacle in American Politics.* Retrieved from The Washington Post: https://www.washingtonpost.com/opinions/the-ugliest-most-appalling-spectacle-in-american-politics/2016/09/05/95179af4-714c-11e6-8365-b19e428a975e_story.html?utm_term=.0a3ec40ba7e0

Saunders, S., & Robers-Davis, T. (2009, April 30). *Porgera in Flames: Barrick-Recommended Military Force Burns Down Hundreds of Homes in PNG.* Retrieved from The San Francisco Bay Area Independent Media Center (Indybay): https://www.indybay.org/newsitems/2009/04/30/18592070.php?show_comments=1

Schwartz, A. (2015, January 26). *The 5 Most Common Unethical Behaviors In the Workplace.* Retrieved from Philadelphia Business Journal: https://www.bizjournals.com/philadelphia/blog/guest-comment/2015/01/most-common-unethical-behaviors-in-the.html

Scott-Morgan, P. (March 1, 1994). The Unwritten Rules of the Game: Master Them, Shatter Them, and Break Through the Barriers to Organizational Change. In P. Scott-Morgan, *The Unwritten Rules of the Game: Master Them, Shatter Them, and Break Through the Barriers to Organizational Change* (p. 256). McGraw Hill.

Seifter, A. (2016, July 25). *At Party Conventions, Big Oil's Media Manipulation Strategy Is On Full Display.* Retrieved from Media

Matters: https://www.mediamatters.org/blog/2016/07/25/party-conventions-big-oil-s-media-manipulation-strategy-full-display/211879

Semuels, A. (2016, July 14). *Poor at 20, Poor for Life.* Retrieved from The Atlantic: https://www.theatlantic.com/business/archive/2016/07/social-mobility-america/491240/

Shapiro, C. (2015). *Corporate Confidential.* St. Martin's Press.

Sibley, A. (2018). *19 Reasons You Should Include Visual Content in Your Marketing.* Retrieved from Hubspot: https://blog.hubspot.com/blog/tabid/6307/bid/33423/19-reasons-you-should-include-visual-content-in-your-marketing-data.aspx

Simons, J. (2016, Aug 9). *Management Style: When Is It Viewed As Abusive?* Retrieved from Wall Street Journal: https://www.wsj.com/articles/management-style-when-is-it-viewed-as-abusive-1470752281

Sina Win, J.D., W. (2011, March 10). *The Red Road Is Not For Sale.* Retrieved from Native Times: https://nativetimes.com/current-news/46-life/commentary/5044-the-red-road-is-not-for-sale

Smith, N. (2012, June 5). *To Build Your Business, Smash Your Silos.* Retrieved from Fast Company: https://www.fastcompany.com/1839317/build-your-business-smash-your-silos

Stebbins, S. (2015, June 29). *The Worst Companies to Work For.* Retrieved from 24/7 Wall Street: http://247wallst.com/special-report/2016/06/10/the-worst-companies-to-work-for-2/

Stillman, J. (2016, July 18). *10 Techniques Used by Manipulators (and How to Fight Them).* Retrieved from Inc.: https://www.inc.com/jessica-stillman/10-popular-techniques-used-by-manipulators-and-how-to-fight-them.html?cid=sf01001&sr_share=twitter

Tiabbi, M. (2013, June 19). *The Last Mystery of the Financial Crisis.* Retrieved from Rolling Stone: https://www.rollingstone.com/politics/news/the-last-mystery-of-the-financial-crisis-20130619

Tierney, J. (2011, August 21). *Do You Suffer From Decision Fatigue.* Retrieved from New York Times: http://www.nytimes.com/2011/08/21/magazine/do-you-suffer-from-decision-fatigue.html

Tweney, D. (2013, May 29). *What's next from Elon Musk? Warp drives, and colonizing Mars.* Retrieved from Venture Beat: https://venturebeat.com/2013/05/29/elon-musk-dreams-big/

Vance, J. (2016, July 30). *Why 'White Trash' Americans Are Flocking to Donald Trump.* Retrieved from New York Post: https://nypost.com/2016/07/30/why-white-trash-americans-are-flocking-to-donald-trump/

Warner, P. (2018). *DecisionWise Benchmark Study Finds that 34% of Employees in the U.S. Do Not Speak Up Because of Fear of Retribution.* Retrieved from Decision Wise: https://www.decision-wise.com/decisionwise-benchmark-study/

World Happiness Report. (2017). Retrieved from World Happiness Report: http://worldhappiness.report

Acknowledgments

THIS BOOK WOULD NOT BE IN YOUR HANDS IF IT WEREN'T FOR A stranger that I met at a conference.

I met Dr. Ade Mabogunje from Stanford University at the Global Innovation Summit in San Jose in 2013. There was a lot of excitement and positivity about innovation at the Summit which I enjoyed immensely. However, at a conference lunch table, I told Ade that I didn't have the same experience as others who were citing fun and success in innovation.

His response? He told me I had to write a book about my experiences. *(What? I'm not a writer!)* He said that my book was "morally necessary" to help other people who struggle to advance ideas.

Now, Ade is someone that I hold in the highest regard. He is incredibly smart, insightful, and inspiring. Disappointing him was never an option. I had never written a book, but he thought I could do it. Therefore, I believed I could do it.

One day, he sent me an article to inspire me. It was written by Dr. Tea Lempiälä, a fellow researcher of his from Finland. Her article, *Corporate Smugglers: Championing Ideas Under the Radar*, was published in Fast Company and was the missing piece of the puzzle. Smuggling. That was it. That is what I was experiencing. That is what I was doing. I wasn't innovating. I was smuggling.

That article changed my life. The word smuggler alone was transformative. I wasn't alone. I realized that there were other people like me struggling inside of companies who were trying to advance their projects. I reached out to Tea immediately, and we became fast friends.

This entire book was inspired by the word Smuggler and her research. (By the way, her dissertation is amazing on the subject: *Entering the Back Stage of Innovation Tensions between the Collaborative Praxis of Idea Development and its Formal Staging in Organizations* can be accessed at http://epub.lib.aalto.fi/pdf/ diss/Aalto_DD_2011_074.pdf. Check it out!) I know that Tea will continue to further the knowledge about Rebels turned Smugglers and how the corporate world might wake up to our strength in promoting healthy change.

Another person who gave me the courage to write this book was my dad, George Neelan. I told my dad that I was going to write this book. He immediately said that he wanted to support me in pursuing my dream. It wasn't a dream as much as it was a decision. But his sentiment was so sincere, so touching, that it meant that I needed to put forth my best effort to make him proud. I needed to publish the best book I could to help the most people. I'm hopeful that I have achieved that goal. I am eternally grateful for his love and support.

From a practical perspective, my mom, Judy and sister, Jennifer, helped me shape my thinking and writing. They also edited a ridiculous amount of work over the course of this project. There is nothing more valuable than feedback from those who aren't afraid to give it to you. If it weren't for them, you would be reading a never-ending run on sentence.

My daughter Bridget was there to support me, especially during setbacks. It was a challenge when I was rejected time and again by agents, or when people would tell me I was crazy for even trying to break into the publishing world. She just kept up with the positive attitude that the book would be published. She never had any doubts.

Mike, my ex-husband, celebrated my successes right along with me. He is one of my biggest cheerleaders. He simply believed in me and supported our little family, and that made me want to do my best.

From the publishing world, I can't tell you how much it means to me that Mark Malatesta my coach, Matthew Carnicelli, my agent, and Lia Ottaviano, my editor, believed in this project. They took the idea, polished it, sold it, and brought it to life. They are the risk takers who had faith in this concept before it was even written.

Finally, I would like to thank my friend Marc Rigby, who was my emotional rock. He was there giving support and advice when the obstacles seemed insurmountable. He would always illuminate my options and his advice was practical and sound. I am fortunate to call him my friend.

It takes a village (of Rebels) after all.

Cheers,
Natalie

NATALIE NEELAN is a longtime entrepreneurial and intrapreneurial strategist who's helped countless white-collar underdogs transform their personal and professional lives via her products, speaking engagements, and blogs. Natalie coaches, consults, and presents to emerging leaders from organizations including Mitsubishi Power, Bayer, Dell, Highmark Blue Cross Blue Shield, PricewaterhouseCoopers, World Health Organization, World Bank, P&G, PNC Bank, Google, HP, and many more.

Natalie has developed practical and immediately implementable approaches to navigate the greatest internal obstacle in bringing initiatives to life—people. She writes with an inimitable sass and blunt practicality that has made her a global influence on innovation strategy and internal adoption.

Ms. Neelan holds an MBA with a concentration in strategy and entrepreneurship from Chatham University and is the founder and president of the Innovation and Strategy firm Straightline. She is based in Pittsburgh, PA. For more, visit natalieneelan.com.

CPSIA information can be obtained
at www.ICGtesting.com
Printed in the USA
BVHW06s0155250418
514362BV00002B/2/P